TO HELL WITH HATE

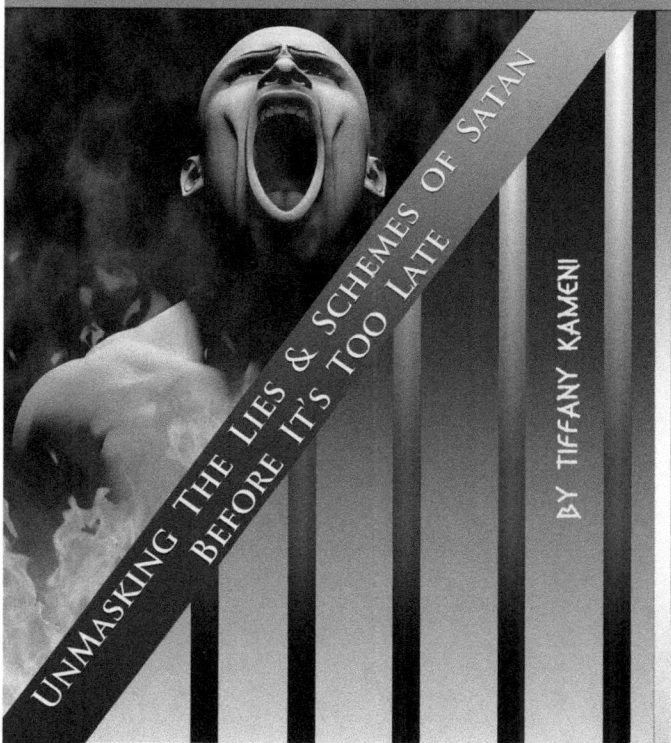

UNMASKING THE LIES & SCHEMES OF SATAN BEFORE IT'S TOO LATE

BY TIFFANY KAMENI

For Prisoners of Hatred
Who Desire to Be Set Free

TO HELL
With Hate

by Tiffany Kameni

To Hell With Hate

Copyright © 2014

Author Tiffany Buckner-Kameni

Email: info@anointedfire.com

Publisher's Website: www.afirepublishing.com or www.anointedfire.com

ISBN-13: 978-0692251232 (Anointed Fire)
ISBN-10: 0692251235

Disclaimer: This book is designed to provide information and motivation to our readers. It is sold with the understanding that the publisher is not engaged to render any type of psychological, legal, or any other kind of professional advice. No warranties or guarantees are expressed or implied by the author, since every man has his own measure of faith. The individual author(s) shall not be liable for any physical, psychological, emotional, financial, or commercial damages, including; but not limited to, special, incidental, consequential or other damages. Our views and rights are the same: You are responsible for your own choices, actions, and results.

The stories in this book are fictional. Names, characters, businesses, places, events and incidents are either the products of the author's imagination or used in a fictitious manner. Any resemblance to actual persons, living or dead, or actual events is purely coincidental.

Note From the Author

When I initially began writing this book, I was writing about all kinds of hatred. I talked about racism, I talked about hatred in the church, and I talked about hatred outside of the church. My goal was to expose hatred for what it was, and that book had plenty of valid points in it, but it wasn't the book GOD wanted me to write. After writing over one hundred pages and then deleting those pages, I came to realize that I was writing on a subject that needed more depth than what I was putting in. I deleted page behind page, hoping that would make the book better, but I had to separate myself from that book to write this one the way GOD wanted me to write. I was able to transfer over much of what I'd written, but many parts of the original book did not make the cut.

GOD began to minister to me, and HE showed me why I couldn't write this book two years ago or even one year ago. It was because I wasn't willing to share my testimony. It wasn't until I was finally ready to share that HE gave me the green light to write this book.

Please know that the purpose of this book is to expose hatred. I am a very private person, but GOD reminded me that my life is not my own. I have to open up so that others who are headed down the paths I've been down may be warned, and some may turn back to CHRIST. For others, this book will serve as a way of escape.

Revelation 12:11: And they overcame him by the blood of the Lamb, and by the word of their testimony; and they loved not their lives unto the death.

I hope and pray that you enjoy this book, and if you are bound by hatred or unforgiveness, I pray that this book is the tool GOD uses to set you free.

Sincerely,
Tiffany Buckner-Kameni

Table of Contents

Introduction

You've been through hurt; you've been betrayed, and if you're still here today, you've lived to tell the story. But the problem today is that many people allow their hurts to drive them down the wrong paths; paths that lead to an eternal separation between them and GOD.

Just what happens when we allow the sun to set on our wrath? What happens when we try to figure out our own way through life?

To Hell with Hate is more than a book written to talk about hatred; it is a book written to pick apart hatred and give you (the reader) a closer look at the twin towers of hatred: selfishness and unforgiveness. After all, we understand what hatred is and what hatred does, but most people don't understand how they got there in the first place. *To Hell with Hate* is a book that delves deep into the roots of hatred, to show you how hatred is formed, why hatred is formed and how to be free from the bondage of hatred.

Way of Escape

I simply knew of GOD, but I did not know
HIM. Sure, I'd been to church a lot as a
child, but after the preacher got through
screaming and jumping around, I would
be sound asleep, wishing he'd hurry up
so we could go home. I saw unholy
religious rituals, but no holiness, so I
attributed church-going people to
hypocrites. But again, I did not know
(knowledge) that being traditionally
religious and being holy were two
different things; one of them being
worldly in nature, and the other being
the very nature of GOD.

I'd been the victim of multiple
molestations as a child. I'd been
molested by some family members and
friends of the family. Because of those
molestations coupled with the
contention-filled environment I grew up

in, a hatred began to grow within me. I hated men, even though I wanted to be married one day. I hated some of my family members. Nevertheless, as a young woman, I discovered a power that I had. The very power that I once detested because it drew perverts to me. I discovered the power of being a woman. My clothes got shorter and my attitude got bigger. I would enter relationship behind relationship, and I thought I had the answer to one of life's biggest mysteries: how to get and keep the man of your dreams. I believed I knew what other women didn't know, and that was how to handle a man. I prided myself on being a woman who could let a man go easily. Every time I saw a woman crying over a man, I would get upset with her. What was wrong with her? Why didn't she understand what I understood? Why didn't she understand or appreciate that she was a woman, and she could call the shots? I became craftier as I tried to figure men out. My relationships would end badly because I wanted a faithful

2

man, but I didn't yet understand that a man must be faithful to GOD before he's able to be faithful to a woman. After all, I wasn't saved, and I thought I'd make someone a great wife.

At the age of seventeen or eighteen, I had a cousin tattoo the word "scandalous" on my right arm. To me, that word represented my distaste for men and what I thought were their ways. That tattoo served as a warning to any man who wanted to enter a relationship with me that I was not the type of woman who would tolerate his foolish ways. Little did I know that the tattoo would only draw the wrong types of men to me.

At home, the fights with my siblings grew more and more violent. We weren't just a family who argued; we were a family who fought hard and often tried to draw blood from one another. We brandished knives, and we said unspeakable evils to each other. There was so much hatred amongst us, and the

3

police department was an all-too-familiar presence at our house. I was ashamed of my family and my family life. I was fighting my brother one day when I was about eight years old, and I don't remember what I said or did, but I do remember my dad crying and asking me why I had so much hatred in me. I was proud of being hateful, so those words were music to my ears. I thought I had to be that way to protect myself from all of the monstrous people who'd hurt me.

I became dominating in relationships. I found that some of the guys who'd flirted with me were actually turned on by my feisty attitude. I didn't understand what I was "turning on" in them, but what I did understand was that being feisty gave me the wheel in those relationships. I was like a chameleon. To some men, I was a cold woman with little tolerance, but to others, I portrayed myself as a shy damsel in distress. I learned to ask questions so I could portray whatever it was I believed that man was looking for.

4

Nevertheless, I could never hide myself for too long, nor could I hide my heart's scars. Anytime I saw what I believed to be signs that the man I was dating was seeing someone else, I would dramatically end the relationship.

After putting on such a show of confidence on the outside, I still had to go back home, close myself in the room and deal with the hurt on the inside. I partied hard with my friends, and I would drink myself into a stupor. Nevertheless, at home, the tears would often flow, and the questions were too many. My past was haunting me, and I didn't know where to go to hide from it. All the same, GOD was tugging on my heart. The pull on me to give myself to HIM was so great, but it was matched by my flesh's desires to remain in the world.

I was always able to silence my convictions temporarily by giving in to my flesh's desires, but the anger and the hatred were eating away at me. The door of escape was wide open for me to go through, but who would lead me through it? All of my friends were worldly. My immediate family was worldly. All of my family who were in church had absolutely nothing to do with us....and quite understandably.

One day, after leaving a club with a friend of mine, I was driving her home when she said to me, "Tiff, we have got to stop this. We need to go to church. I've been feeling really bad lately." It felt so good to hear her say those words because I had that same tugging going on in my heart. We talked about it and agreed to go to her aunt's church the next day.

When I walked into the church, I immediately knew that it was the church GOD wanted me to go to. I felt peaceful there. I felt loved and welcomed. My friend and I both decided that day that we would be joining that church after a few visits, and we did.

I thought going to church would change me immediately, but change takes time. I was hurt when I noticed those same fiery lusts that once overtook me were still in me. Those desires to sin were still there. At that time, I didn't understand that the mind has to be changed by the bringing in of the WORD of GOD. I wasn't reading my Bible too much at home. I opened my Bible on Sundays and Tuesdays only, during church service or Bible study.

Because I wasn't that into the WORD, the WORD was not yet in me; therefore, I continued to think the same way I thought while in the world. I fought hard to stop fornicating, and I fought hard to stop living a lifestyle I knew GOD wasn't pleased with, but I didn't know how to stop.

This is what happens to us as believers. A believer who does not give their hearts to GOD and take the WORD of GOD into their hearts is a believer who will continue to head down the wrong roads of life. Additionally, that same believer will likely blame or question GOD any time the life he (or she) has been building for himself (or herself) crumbles in the hands of a trial. Those wrong roads that we take often take us through so much pain that, in addition to having to get delivered from the bad situations we enter, we often have to get delivered from the wrongful thinking we've picked up along the way. It is that wrongful thinking that leads us to hate in the first place.

Every road I'd taken, I'd witnessed GOD open a way of escape for me, but the problem was, I didn't think I needed rescuing, so I continued down those roads until the truth sent me running back to my FATHER. Before you enter into relationships and situations that lead to heartbreak, GOD will open a door for you. HE will provide a way of escape for you, but if you don't take that door when it's opened, you may not get a second chance to go through it. Such was the case of two of my mother's brothers. They'd both died trying to hold on to adulterous women. One of my uncles had been kicked out of his own home by his wife, who then moved another man in. His new house suspiciously caught on fire while he and his son were sleeping, and he died saving his son's life. The other uncle had gotten drunk and allegedly gotten into an argument with his wife about sex. I'm not sure what happened, but the story was that he'd broken a few things in the house and left. His wife called the police, who came out and found him crouching behind a trash can. The police told him to come out with his hands up, but he kept his hands in his pockets. That's because he was drunk and probably thought he could approach the officers and reason with them. Instead, they opened fire and killed him. He wasn't a criminal; he was a man who'd made some pretty bad relationship choices, and he paid for it with his life.

Of course, the officers didn't find a weapon on him and justified the shooting by saying his hands were in his pocket.

The point is: GOD is still faithful, but we need to embrace faith if we want to stay out of situations that lead us towards death, hatred and pain. We are the ones who put ourselves in these situations, not GOD. We are the ones who stay in dangerous places thinking we can clean them up. Both of my uncles had seen the signs that the women they were with were not wife-worthy, but they stayed anyway. Had my uncles went through those doors of escape, they would probably be alive today.

Little did I know that I'd repeat those same bad choices when entering relationships with men. Little did I know that I needed to be delivered from wrongful thinking and then wait on GOD to send my spouse to me. Because I didn't understand that I was not to

10

choose a man for myself, I ended up
following that same path I'd seen so
many people in my family travel before;
some of them having returned, while
some of them having perished along the
way.

I want you to see the patterns in each
story and not so much the offenders.
You see, we often pay so much negative
attention to the offenders that we don't
take the time out to rebuke the people
who opened themselves up for these
offenders in the first place. There are
tons of evil people in the world, and we
can't say they deserve to be stoned just
because they unleashed their evil into
our lives; especially, if we've invited them
into our lives.
Each testimony I share with you has an
offender and a defender, but pay
attention to the defender. Ask yourself
why they were in those situations in the
first place. The goal is to learn to be
accountable for our own wrongs so we'll
stop going into bad situations and

blowing the siren. I refuse to blame the people who hurt me for hurting me. They were who they were before I met them, but I share my testimony to help others understand that there is no right way to do wrong and there are no blessings in sin. If you want to stay in love and go to Heaven, you must first stop entering sin and living in hell.

Getting Back to the Root

I couldn't look at his face anymore. I was tired of being fondled by him. I was tired of freezing in fear every time he caught me alone somewhere in the house.

I was 12-years-old, and he was my Daddy's friend. I'd known him since I was born, and I had always seen him as an uncle. That was until he decided to change my view of him. I was a pre-teen, just entering puberty, and all of a sudden his view of me changed. I was no longer the little girl he'd defend, give candy to or give a piggy back ride to. I was beginning to fill out, and he noticed.

There I was in the kitchen with him, and my heart was racing. I was taught to be respectful towards adults, and I didn't

13

know how to tell him that his advances were unwanted. I feared what would happen next, so I froze. I stood there as he fondled me. I numbed myself to the pain of his hand touching me where I did not want to be touched. But just as fast as it started, it ended. One of my siblings could be heard coming down the hall, and I was so thankful. *I'll have to be more careful next time*, I told myself. I'd learned to dodge him by following my siblings around any time he came over for a visit.

This went on for two years. I learned how to maneuver myself out of private places when he came over. I was too afraid to tell my parents; after all, he was my daddy's best friend. At the same time, being molested wasn't new to me. I'd learned earlier of the dangers of being a young woman, and I'd gotten pretty good at identifying what I referred to as "the sleepy look." The "sleepy look" to me was when a man would begin to look sleepy when he was alone with me. This look indicated to me that he was about to touch me; therefore, I learned how to avoid being alone with men. Whenever I did get caught by a man in a private place, I'd learned to be crafty to rescue myself. As much as I loved being a girl, I hated having girl parts. After all, they were a magnet for the creepiest and most wicked of men.

At the age of 14, I decided to blow the whistle on my dad's friend. We'll call him Ramsey. He'd called my parents house looking for my Dad, and I had the misfortune of answering the telephone. There was no caller identification back then; all you had was hope. When I heard his voice, that paralyzing fear came in again. I looked around for my brother and sister because I wanted him to hear their voices. That way, he wouldn't talk perverted to me again. But they were outside and the silence in the background was a big giveaway. After all, he'd known them since they were babies as well. He knew how loud they were, and he knew that I was obviously home alone. "Let me talk with your dad," he murmured. I looked out the living room door, hoping to see my sister or brother. I wanted to motion for them to come into the house, but they were nowhere in sight.

"He's not home yet, but he'll be here soon," I responded. His voice got quieter, softer, like a scary whisper.

"Is your mom home?" My heart raced as I tried to think up a quick lie, but it wouldn't come out.

"No, she's not home yet either." That was it. That was all he'd wanted to hear. He said the words that terrified me to the point of no return.

"Tiffany, I am attracted to you, and you know it. You are not a little girl anymore. You are a woman, and I want to make you my woman. I want you to meet me at the corner store in twenty-minutes. I have a house that your dad doesn't know about. I want to move you in with me, and I will take care of you. I'll buy you anything you want, you won't have to go to school anymore, and I'll teach you how to drive. You don't have to bring any of your clothes with you; I'll buy you a whole new wardrobe. Just meet me at the store in twenty minutes, okay?" I could barely breathe. The fear was too much, but I got up enough breath to muster out an "okay," and with that, we hung up the line. I began to pace back and forth as fear flooded my mind. I wasn't attracted to him. After all, he was forty-something years old, and I was only fourteen. He had gone too far, in my mind. Now, he was planning to kidnap me and hide me from my parents. Even though I knew there was no way I would meet him at the store, I feared what he would do next. If he got me out of my parents' sight, what would he do to me? I feared the worst.

Suddenly, the front door opened and my parents came in. I couldn't hold it anymore, and I belted it out. I told them everything he'd said. They both stood there in shock. My dad went immediately to the phone to call him, and my mom started asking me questions. I shivered and cried as I recalled the last two years of horror to her. What was going to happen now? After all, he'd been my dad's best friend since before I was born.

I went to my bedroom and paced, my stomach churning with anguish and fear. I bit my fingernails as I walked back and forth, fearing what would happen next. My mom came to the door, and my worst fears were confirmed. She said that Ramsey claimed he was just joking with me. He wasn't serious at all. I pleaded my case again. He wasn't playing. He'd been touching me for two years. My voice was loud and quivering. I could hear my dad yelling and crying as he talked to Ramsey. I didn't know how it would all end, but I had a bad feeling it would not work out in my favor. I was right.

The next day, I came home from school, and Ramsey was sitting in the living room. He wouldn't look at me, and I was too afraid to look at him. I rushed to my bedroom, closed my door and began to cry. I found myself pacing back and forth again, and then my bedroom door opened. It was my dad. "Baby, please forgive me. He came by so we could talk. He said he was just playing with you; he wasn't serious." Once again, I pleaded my case. This man had been putting his hand in my undergarments for two years. How was that a joke? I cried as I yelled the facts to my dad. He responded by telling me that Ramsey had threatened to kill himself, and that's why he invited

him over. I was horrified, and I drew
back what felt like the last of my
strength as I exclaimed, "Most dads
would have volunteered to do it for him!
He wouldn't have to kill himself!"

I had every reason to hate that man. I
had every reason to hate my parents.
This wasn't the first time I'd felt
betrayed. Why wasn't anyone fighting
for me? After all of those years and
countless molestations by family
members, I'd finally opened my mouth to
tell someone about a molestation I was
enduring. I'd moved past the fears that
had kept me silent ever since I was a
baby, but my worst fears were confirmed.
No one was going to do anything about
it, so it was better for me to just be quiet
and keep dodging the perverts.

I began to despise men, all the while
wanting to have a boyfriend. But in
order for me to be involved with
someone, I felt I had to be in control.

After all, my perception of men had changed. They were no longer protectors and providers. To me, they were monsters. Sure, I was still attracted to them, but I found myself falling in love with characters from my television screen. After all, they were protective, loving and fearless.

I had every reason to justify hating others, and I did. I hated a certain type of man, and I became very discerning. I could identify a pervert from a mile away, just by the way he looked at me when no one else was looking his way. Like most women, I began to develop a "type" in regards to men. I loathed sexual perverts and would often lash out at them. Every woman needs a man to stand in as a role model to show her what a husband should look like, but since I didn't have one, I turned to television and picked out role models from there.

Additionally, I began to stay away from home longer, often adopting surrogate families where I felt protected. The mother of one of my closest friends took me under her wings, and her family welcomed me with open arms. From that moment on, I spent almost every day after school at their house. Not only did they appear to be protective of me, they were protective of me in relation to my own family, and I felt safe at their place.

The hatred continued to grow, but I didn't realize it was there. I just thought I was "too smart" for silly men. I thought some men (types) deserved to be mistreated, and I was all-too-willing to take on the job of mistreating them. Noticing what appeared to be conceit and lack of tolerance towards men, a lot of hurting women became drawn to me. They loved how brazen I was with men. After all, many of my friends were settling down, falling in love and having children, but I was too busy letting R. Kelly tell me what to look for. Music videos were like my own version of church. After listening to certain songs for a while, I thought I knew how to handle the next guy who blindly wanted to be in a relationship with me. I got louder, my clothes became skimpier, and my choices became more and more reckless.

Hatred took me down some dark paths, but the amazing thing was that I was able to function and not realize I was living in a state of hatefulness. One of the things about hate is that it can often mask itself. When we hear the word "hate", we often think of someone who's walking around mad, but that's not always the case. I actually hid my hatred behind a smile. I was always considered super sweet, and people often told me how sweet I was every time they saw me. People often asked me how it was that every time they saw me, I was smiling.

That's because I was plotting something in my then warped mind. I was intelligent, young and crafty.

Anytime hatred sits in a person's heart, that person becomes better and better at hiding it. I've noticed that hatred often masks itself well in young people, but in older people, it doesn't hide itself very well. I've also noticed that Satan likes to attack us when we are young. It's amazing how the monsters in movies had a heart when it came to children (except Freddy Krueger, of course), but real-life monsters are heartless. That's because real-life monsters have a job of creating miniature monsters who are set to grow up to become even bigger monsters.

A few years after I'd blown the whistle on Ramsey, my parents divorced. To say I was happy about the divorce is an understatement. I was thrilled that my dad was moving out because that meant I wouldn't see Ramsey anymore. It also meant that he'd likely take my brother with him, and that seemed like a dream come true for me. The day I heard my parents were divorcing, I went around telling my friends that I was throwing a party at my mother's house. I wanted to celebrate because I thought things would get easier from there.

How did hatred form in me? Hatred entered me through pain. Pain is hatred's favorite entry door. That's why GOD tells us not to let the sun set on our wrath. In other words, be angry, but don't stay there for too long. Sitting in that pain only makes you marinate in that pain. It took years, salvation and the WORD of GOD to deliver me from all that hurt and pain, but one of the greatest realizations I've come to over the years is: You can't change what a person is, and you shouldn't invite a devil-filled character into your life. I went through my party stages, and I went through a promiscuity stage because I didn't love myself. I had never witnessed another human being truly loving me, so I didn't know how to love myself. I thought life was about me getting what I wanted so I could finally be happy. I often worried that I would repeat the mistakes my parents had made with me, so anytime I thought I was pregnant, I would throw myself on the arm of the couch. I tried to annihilate any life that I thought was growing in me because I didn't want that child to enter into a world with me as its mother. But one day, something miraculous happened. I got married to a man who had two children. That marriage was my first marriage, and by that time, I'd started going to church and had gotten saved. My husband's oldest son was only three-years-old when he came to live with us. I'd spoken with my husband and his son's mother about discipline, and they both gave me the green light to discipline the child. I witnessed myself

being a great mother to him. I
disciplined him and loved him as if he
was my own. I saw in me something
foreign. I saw me being the parent I'd
wished I had.

One of the memories that is burned into
my imagination is a particular night
when we had all gone to bed. My
stepson was four-years-old by then, and
was asleep in his room when we
suddenly received a phone call. It was
almost twelve in the morning, and we'd
received news that one of my husband's
relatives had left her son at the movies.
He'd tried to reach her, but she wasn't
answering her phone. The story was
that she'd gone to the movies with her
sixteen-year-old son and left with some
strange guy. The caller informed us that
the sixteen-year-old was the only person
left at the theater and didn't have a ride
home. They'd called us because we lived
right around the corner from the theater.
My husband volunteered to go and pick

him up while I stayed in the bed.
It wasn't long before he returned and got
back in the bed with me. I asked my
husband where his sixteen-year-old
cousin was, and he said he was in my
stepson's room. He'd be sleeping there
for the night. Before I could think
straight, I sat up in the bed and said, "Go
and get my baby! Bring him in here!"
My husband looked at me and told me to
lie back down. He assured me that all
would be okay. His son was in the top
bunk and his cousin was in the bottom
bunk. My voice got louder as I
remembered all of the times I had been
molested or fondled. "Go get my baby!" I
exclaimed. Finally, he got up and went to
bring the child into our room. He placed
him in the bed, and I slept peacefully
after that.

One day, the LORD brought that story
back to my remembrance. I was nothing
like my parents. I was loving and
protective over the life that was in my

care. I'd truly forgotten that he was my stepson, and I saw him as my own child. He would always come to me to tell me whatever he was afraid to tell his father. We had our inside jokes, and we'd often laugh about how predictable his father was. When my marriage ended with his father, my greatest pain and fear was losing contact with the son I'd grown to love. For a long time, I couldn't reach him, and for a long time, my friends told me to just let it go. They often reminded me that he wasn't my blood, but that didn't matter to me. He was my baby. Years later, he went to his grandmother's house and asked if she'd call me. She did and she told me how much he loved to talk about me. She said to me that he was visiting her house, and I could come and pick him up if I wanted to, but it had to be our secret. His parents would likely not be too happy about him being with me.

When I went to pick him up, I saw this tall guy walking out of the house. It was hard enough trying to believe that the deep-voiced guy on the other end of the phone line was my baby in teenage form, but to see this tall version of him walking towards me was beyond what I could express in words. We hugged and we've since kept in contact over the years.

Hatred didn't win. Even though I'm not a mother as of yet, I am a changed character. The old person has died. Hatred no longer lives in or with me, and I've made some wonderful plans for my children when they come here. All the same, anytime I see someone who is hateful, I know that there's a story there, and I can empathize with them more than others can. I know that monsters weren't born; they were created.

Years later, I told my parents about their parenting and the things I'd endured growing up under them, and they both apologized. My dad told me that he'd seen Ramsey, and he'd become wrathful when he saw him, but of course, it was far too late for that. I told him that I'd forgiven Ramsey and I have. Why did I forgive a man who tried to fondle and kidnap me? Because I have to believe that he is not the same man anymore and that he regrets what he's done. I have many regrets from the lifestyle I lived when I was a sinner, and GOD has forgiven me. Who am I to not forgive Ramsey or the people who've hurt me? Even if Ramsey hasn't changed, he's no longer my problem. I can only pray that he gives himself to the LORD before it's too late.

Hatred...Behind the Mask

I remember begging for a man I'd once thought to be my friend to let me up. I was nineteen years old, unsaved, naïve, and at that moment, I was being attacked. A man I thought was a friend was trying to rape me. At that time, I was engaged to get married, but I'd let an old friend of mine talk me into visiting him. He told me that he had brought me back some jewelry from overseas. He knew that my weakness was material things. With little to no wisdom in store, I went to his house thinking that I was going to get my free jewelry and go on with my life. Instead, when I got there, he invited me to his bedroom. I didn't want to go, but there were two women in the living room smoking marijuana and I didn't want to smell it, so I followed him thinking I'd go in and he'd hand me the

33

jewelry. My plan was to talk to him for about ten minutes and then leave.

After entering his room, he insisted that I take a seat while he got the jewelry. He sat down next to me and began saying that he just wanted to have a conversation with me before giving me the jewelry. He was in the military and hadn't seen me in two years, so he kept saying that he missed me and only wanted to talk with me before I left. He then started trying to close the bedroom door, and I kept extending my leg to keep the door from closing. I was absolutely determined to be faithful to the man I'd casually promised to marry.

My attacker was at least 6'2"and made of solid muscle, while I was 5'0 and about 100 to 110 pounds. He violently snatched my leg, closed the door and started his attack. At first, I thought he was just playfully, but aggressively, making a move on me, but when I caught a glimpse of his eyes, I realized I was in trouble. His eyes were dark and his face looked familiar, but changed. He was screaming something, but I couldn't make out his words because I was distracted by the saliva that was spraying from his mouth as he yelled. I thought I was going to die that day, but I was very determined to survive. I locked my legs, and at first, I demanded that he let me up. I began using all kinds of vulgar language hoping to scare him off me, but he became increasingly upset, and I realized I was no longer dealing with him; I was battling with something evil. I then started begging him to let me go. I tried to fight, but I was not even close to being a match to him. He kept mumbling on and on about how I'd been a tease all those years, so he said he was going to "take it." In other words, he was going to rape me. I screamed for the girls in the living room to come and help me, but when I did, he took his forearm and placed it on my neck. He began to press down into my neck with his forearm until I couldn't scream anymore. He demanded that I "shut up," and he threatened to kill me if I didn't release the lock I had on my legs, but I was unrelenting. I was determined not to be raped again. I had spent my life being molested and had been raped before, so I was at an age where I was determined to not let it happen to me again. I kept my legs locked, and as strong as he was, he couldn't pry them open. This battle went on for more than thirty minutes, and of course the girls never came to my aid. To this day, I'm not sure if they'd left the house before or during the attack, but when it was over, I didn't see them. I kept begging him to let me go, and then I started lying. I told him that I had to pick my sister up from school, but he ignored me. It was as if he wasn't there. His eyes were dark and he was demonically set on one purpose ... getting my clothes off to rape me. Throughout the attack, he would press his forearm into my neck repeatedly, trying to get me to release the lock I had on my legs and to stop screaming. Honestly, there were times I didn't realize I was screaming until he'd start strangling me again and telling me to shut up.

After that long wrestling match, he managed to get my jeans off; nevertheless, I locked my legs again and he couldn't get them open. He exposed himself somehow and tried to find a way to rape me, but the lock on my legs and the way I kept twisting my body made it impossible for him. Finally, he got tired of trying and told me that I was lucky. He said that all of that fighting with me had turned him off. He then got up and started pacing back and forth. I could tell he was contemplating his next move. Suddenly, I could see fear in his eyes as it became real to him the horror of what had just happened. It was as real as the redness around my neck. Fear had me in its grips as well because I didn't know what was going on in his warped mind, but I knew it wasn't good.

My attacker began to apologize and plead with me for forgiveness. He started lying and saying he only had six months to live. He said the doctors had found a tumor on his heart, and he was determined to "procreate" and thought I would make a great mother. He said he'd thought about making me a mother while stationed in Germany. I pretended to understand his story, and I pretended to believe him because I was in survival mode. I wanted to survive and I believed that he was thinking about killing me. As we walked down the hall towards the living room, he'd placed his hands on the back of my neck. His hands felt unsure as he kept moving them up and down my neck as if he was wrestling with the thoughts of breaking my neck. I walked faster and reached up to hold his hands in a comforting way. I wanted him to think that everything was okay.

I don't remember praying; I just remember trying to get to the front door. After unsuccessfully trying to give me a ring off his finger (I kept denying it), he finally let me leave, apologizing continuously as I exited the door. When I got out of his front door, I took off running towards my car as he stood in the doorway looking fearful. I got into my car, locked the doors, and pulled away crying. I was frantic when I got home and told my mother about the attack. She asked me if I wanted to call the police, and I responded with a resounding no. I knew that going to court with him would be no easy task. I knew they would ask me why I'd gone to his bedroom if I wasn't expecting sex. I thought about all of the horrible things that would be said about me.

It took years to heal from that attack, and the many attacks I'd gone through over the course of my life. I was broken, and I was living continuously as a victim. Because of the pain I'd endured, I continued to victimize any man who dared to call himself my boyfriend. I thought I was finally in control of my life because as an adult, I had the power to say who I wanted to be with and who couldn't come near me. I was a fighter, but I was fighting the wrong battle.

Forgiveness is necessary, but it is easier to forgive someone when you get a better understanding of the WORD of GOD. It was easier for me to forgive when I accepted my responsibility in the crime against myself. I put myself in harm's way by chasing material things. What did that situation do for me?

1. It made me realize that I was truly loved. You see, GOD protected me from a man who I AM SURE was thinking about harming me that day.
2. It made me a better wife. When I

got married, I knew that I couldn't hang out with men; especially any who'd shown any type of romantic interest in me at some point.

3. It made me stronger. I have survived a lot, but only by the grace of GOD.

4. It gave me another reason to stand in awe of GOD. Let's face it; HE protected me that day and throughout my life.

5. It made me go through forgiveness training. It forced me to question why forgiveness was necessary, and then I learned to seek it.

6. It made me a better mother. Even though I haven't birthed any children of my own yet, I have vowed in my heart to protect my children from the very things I was once exposed to.

7. It gave me a testimony, and with my testimony, many are able to find the courage to be set free in CHRIST JESUS. My testimonies

are my belt's notches because they give me extra leverage against the enemy.

8. It gave me the ability to relate to people who are often judged by the traditional church. I see and love those souls who want out of that lifestyle but just don't know how to exist or if they can exist in this whole new mindset that the WORD tells them about. I'm a living testimony that they can.

9. It helped me to see what was important in my life and what was not. I learned not to be so materialistic because I'd almost given my life for a few pieces of jewelry. By the way, there was no jewelry to be had.

10. It likely saved my life. You see, that situation made me more aware of what could happen to me, so I stopped doing many of the reckless things I'd enjoyed.

11. It gave me a preview of myself as a

wife. My two reasons for fighting off that rape were because I didn't want to be a victim again, and I wanted to be faithful to my then fiance.

Of course, it didn't change my view of men at that time. It took the WORD to come into me to evict all of that foolishness out of me, but eventually I surrendered myself to GOD and started my journey from who I was to the Great I AM.

Why was I attacked so much by men? Why were most of the crimes against me sexual in nature? It all goes back to the earlier times when the Bible was being written. In most of the cases when a kingdom attacked another kingdom, the attackers would kill the men and make concubines of the women. Most crimes against women are sexual in nature. That's because the enemy understands soul ties and what they do to women. A

43

woman can self-destruct from within if she's not delivered from soul ties, fear and hurt. At the same time, the LORD told me the enemy attacked me because of who I am in HIM. The devil was trying to remove every trace of GOD he saw in me, but no matter what I'd been through, and no matter how far I went away from GOD, I still hungered for my FATHER in Heaven. There were many days that I would curl up and cry out to HIM. After sifting me, the enemy still saw traces of GOD in me, and he fought with all of his might to remove GOD'S likeness from me. The love that was in my heart was far more rooted than the hatred that was covering my heart. Hatred was never able to fully penetrate me. Instead, like the would-be rapist, hatred held me down and tried to choke the life out of me, but GOD was with me. HE continued to rescue me again and again, and I began to recognize that HE was protecting me. Many days, I drove home in tears after having sinned with a "boyfriend." Many days, I'd gone to my knees and begged GOD to forgive and deliver me. The enemy just could not stop me from praying. He could not stop me from wanting to find my way back to my FATHER.

Why does the enemy attack you so viciously? The enemy fights when he sees hope in you, an anointing on you and GOD standing up for you. When he asked to sift Peter, he was asking to look for sin in Peter. He wanted to remove every resemblance of GOD from Peter. He wanted to try Peter, and to try him meant to take him through pain. That's what the enemy does to us. He tries us just as he tried Job. His goal is to get us to curse GOD, denounce GOD and to follow after the kingdom of darkness. The enemy uses pain as a recruiting method to enlist men and women for his army. He knows that flesh has no inheritance with GOD, so his plan is to get people to fight against people. But even when a person serves Satan, he still hates them because they are loved by GOD; therefore, he uses them and then disposes of them. He takes that hurt little girl and continues to hurt her until she grows up to be a mother. She will then inflict the very hurt on her children that was inflicted upon her. Her children will likely grow up and inflict that very same pain on their own children, and the cycle will continue. In addition to hurting her own children, that woman will go out and hurt anyone who dares allow her near their heart. Because of her hurt and hatred, she has unknowingly become a recruiter for Satan's army. She collects the souls of the men who dare to lie with her. Anytime she meets a decent man, she hurts him again and again until he begins to believe that all women are wicked and don't like good men. He then becomes the heartless monster she's taught him to be, and he goes about doing to other women what his recruiter

has done to him....and the cycle
continues.

Layers

With all the things that we endure in life,
it is no wonder that hatred tends to form
in layers. It is very hard to reach a man
who's been repeatedly hurt because each
layer of his pain represents an external
skeleton, one he uses to guard his heart.
But guarding his heart is of no value
when it's full of hate. That's because
he's accepted hatred as his normal, and
he rejects love from coming in to evict
the hatred that's in him. To a person full
of hatred, love doesn't exist, and if it
does, it's allergic to them. They go from
relationship to relationship expecting
the worst, and each time they are
betrayed, another layer forms on top of
their already hardened hearts. Any
person who dares to get past those
layers and enter a hateful man's heart
will find out just how hard it is to get

away from that man. That's why we have to be careful as to whose heart we attempt to win.

Some of the layers of hatred are:
- Fear
- Anger
- Unforgiveness
- Pride
- Unlearned Lessons
- Humiliation
- Self-Pity
- Envy & Jealousy
- Selfish Ambition
- Lack of Knowledge & Understanding

Fear

Fear is the opposite of faith when used improperly. The only fear that's legal in the earth and spirit realm is the fear of GOD. The fear of GOD is an extension of faith. Anytime we fear someone other than GOD, we are in the same saying that we believe the person can do exceeding abundantly above all that we ask or think, according to the power that works in them, when a greater Power is in operation from within us. What happens is, we take the scriptures and turn them around, giving the enemy what belongs to GOD. Fear is a form of reverence, and we should only reverence the LORD.

Needless to say, we often fear mankind because of what we've seen mankind do to one another. Additionally, we've been hurt by other humans, so we know that a person whose heart is set on breaking us will do as much as they can to reach their goals. With that said, fear is usually a direct result of the hurt we have endured. Fear serves as a warning to us, giving us an imaginative view of what could happen to us. We see this possibility and attempt to take the necessary precautions to avoid being ensnared by the very thing or person we fear. Because of this, man often hates what he fears.

Proverbs 1:7: The fear of the LORD *is* the beginning of knowledge: *but* fools despise wisdom and instruction.
Proverbs 9:10: The fear of the LORD *is* the beginning of wisdom: and the knowledge of the holy *is* understanding.
Psalm 56:11: In God have I put my trust: I will not be afraid what man can do unto me.
Matthew 10:28: And fear not them which kill the body, but are not able to kill the soul: but rather fear him which is able to destroy both soul and body in hell.

Anger

Anger usually sets in when a fear has been realized. Anger is our soul's response to being mishandled or our heart's response to being deceived. To be angry means to be wrathful and full of indignation. Anger is a form of pride, but GOD allows us to be angry for a little while. After all, we are made in HIS image, but we are not allowed to let the sun set on our wrath. Wrath is anger in

action. It is to be moved by the anger
from within. To be wrathful is to
respond with anger to the person or
thing that's upset you, whether your
response is verbal or non-verbal. GOD
told us not to let the sun set on our
wrath. The reason for this
commandment is that any thoughts we
allow to sit on our hearts will eventually
make their way into our hearts. Wrath
should not be a lifestyle; anger should be
a momentary feeling that reminds us
that we are human.

If we allow our hearts to marinate in
anger for more than a day, our hearts will
harden, and it is then that anger turns
into unforgiveness. Unforgiveness
means to be extensively angry and
wrathful.

Ephesians 4:26: Be ye angry, and sin not:
let not the sun go down upon your
wrath: Neither give place to the devil.
Psalm 103:9: He will not always chide:
neither will he keep his anger for ever.
Isaiah 57:16: For I will not contend for

ever, neither will I be always wroth: for
the spirit should fail before me, and the
souls which I have made.

Matthew 5:24: Leave there thy gift before
the altar, and go thy way; first be
reconciled to thy brother, and then come
and offer thy gift.

Unforgiveness

GOD made us in HIS likeness, and one of
the things you'll notice about HIS
commandments to us is that they are
designed to encourage us to behave like
HIM. GOD forgave us for our sins. As a
matter of fact, HE sent HIS only
Begotten Son to live for us and die for
our sins. It is a direct insult to GOD for
a man to seek forgiveness from the
LORD but refuse to forgive his brethren.
To do so is to exalt one's self in pride
above the WORD of GOD.

Unforgiveness is one of the most potent
ingredients in hatred. To be extensively
angry with someone is to be unlike GOD,

and more like Satan. Think about it this way: Have you ever been angry with someone after finding out something they did that directly affected you? Do you remember how you responded to that anger, but when the anger subsided, you went back and apologized for overreacting? That's because you were able to think with a sound mind the minute wrath left you. Now, imagine living in that angry state of mind extensively. This means that you trade your peace for wrath, and because wrath takes you out of GOD'S will, it takes you from under the protective covering of GOD and exposes you to the demonic. Anyone who comes outside of the will of GOD will slowly begin to look more like GOD'S enemy and less like the LORD. **Matthew 6:15:** But if ye forgive not men their trespasses, neither will your Father forgive your trespasses.
Luke 17:3: Take heed to yourselves: If thy brother trespass against thee, rebuke him; and if he repent, forgive him.

Matthew 18:21-22: Then came Peter to him, and said, Lord, how oft shall my brother sin against me, and I forgive him? Till seven times? Jesus saith unto him, I say not unto thee, Until seven times: but, Until seventy times seven.

Pride

Pride is triggered by a haughty spirit. Pride is when man hardens his heart and begins to become inflated by lies. Pride is when a man refuses to humble himself before the LORD. It means to directly rebel against GOD. Pride occurs when a man settles in his heart that he will walk, do and think a certain way, outside of the will of GOD. Of all the things found in hatred, pride is one stance that provokes GOD to wrath.

Proverbs 16:18: Pride goeth before destruction, and an haughty spirit before a fall.

Proverbs 6:16-19: These six things does the LORD hate: yea, seven are an abomination unto him:

A proud look, a lying tongue, and hands that shed innocent blood,

A heart that devises wicked imaginations, feet that are swift in running to evil,

A false witness that speaks lies, and he that sows discord among brethren.

Unlearned Lessons

Anytime we go to school, we go to learn many lessons. Each lesson is designed to help us advance to the next level. As you advance in school, you'll find that many of the topics are not required to graduate, and you'll likely stay away from topics and classes that do not benefit you. For example, if your goal is to become a doctor, you will likely decide against participating in any of the Creative Writing classes.
The same goes for life. Every relationship we have is either GOD-approved or in direct opposition to GOD. One of the most effective ways to

determine whether a relationship is GOD'S will for you is to check the fruit of the relationship. What's being born of that relationship? If it's constant bickering, wrath and stunts in jail, chances are, that relationship is against GOD.

Hatred sits in the midst of wrongful relationships because wrongful relationships stir up strife. Strife is a demonic environment in which every dark thing can exist. But the problem with many of us believers is, we don't know when and how to let go of relationships that keep us in offense and strife. Instead, we try to find ways to hold onto the very relationships GOD is telling us to let go of. Because of this, people who stay in bad relationships with friends, family and romantic interests often live in the midst of anger, strife and everything that comes with the two. They become familiar with anger, pride, unforgiveness and every spirit that comes with them. In other words, they begin to accept, live with and become comfortable with familiar spirits. The WORD tells us that if our right hand offends our left hand, to cut it off. What this means is that if someone is in our lives and they are an offense to our lives and our purposes, cut them off; otherwise, they're going to help you develop some evil habits that will keep you out of GOD'S will and away from your blessings. If your brother offends you, you have to forgive him, but if your brother constantly offends you, you may want to consider doing as Abraham did with Lot: Send him in a different direction.

Matthew 18:8-9: Wherefore if thy hand or thy foot offend thee, cut them off, and cast them from thee: it is better for thee to enter into life halt or maimed, rather than having two hands or two feet to be cast into everlasting fire. And if thine eye offend thee, pluck it out, and cast it from thee: it is better for thee to enter into life with one eye, rather than having two eyes to be cast into hell fire.

Psalm 26:4: I have not sat with vain persons, neither will I go in with dissemblers.

Psalm 106:43: Many times did he deliver them; but they provoked him with their counsel, and were brought low for their iniquity.

Humiliation

Humiliation is to be made aware of the fact that you are human. It is to be humbled by suffering through embarrassment. To be humiliated is to have your pride deflated or your fears inflated in the presence of others. Humiliation often provokes extreme wrath, and oftentimes, it provokes vengeance in a person. We are creatures who either want to fit in with the crowd comfortably or stand out in a good way. When we've been humiliated, it is harder for us to forgive the person who's humiliated us because they've caused us to stand out in a bad way. We were uncovered and vulnerable, and we won't be comfortable being in the midst of the people who've seen us in such a state. When Ham saw his father (Noah) drunk and uncovered, he was supposed to cover his father. Instead, he exposed him. Shem and Japheth came in and covered Noah, and the scriptures tell us that when Noah woke up, he was angry with Ham and cursed him. Noah was a man of GOD, but at the same time, Noah was human. Anyone who humiliates a man or woman of GOD is attempting to discredit their ministry by showing others that the person being humiliated is nothing more than a mere human being.

Philippians 2:3: Let nothing be done through strife or vainglory; but in lowliness of mind let each esteem other better than themselves.

Luke 14:8-11: When thou art bidden of any man to a wedding, sit not down in the highest room; lest a more honourable man than thou be bidden of him; And he that bade thee and him come and say to thee, Give this man place; and thou begin with shame to take the lowest room. But when thou art bidden, go and sit down in the lowest room; that when he that bade thee cometh, he may say unto thee, Friend, go up higher: then shalt thou have worship in the presence of them that sit at meat with thee. For whosoever exalteth himself shall be abased; and he that humbleth himself shall be exalted.

Self-Pity

Self-pity is a form of conceit. It is to consider your own pain while disregarding the lesson in that pain. GOD told us to love others as we love ourselves, but with self-pity, we take our eyes off our brethren, and we begin to feed our pain and nurse our pride. It's okay to be hurt, but to pity one's self extensively is to try and look at that hurt from another angle; an angle that helps to keep you in unforgiveness and to keep you acting and thinking like a victim. In CHRIST, we are more than conquerors. You'll notice that people who often indulge in self-pity eventually become pitiful. Merriam-Webster defines "pitiful" as: (1) deserving or causing feelings of pity or sympathy. (2) causing feelings of dislike or disgust by not being enough or not being good enough.

Self-pity causes us to sit in pain for too long, thus beginning to diminish who we are to deal with our wounds.

Anytime we sit in pain too long, we will eventually hate whoever caused us to be in pain.

Matthew 11:28-30: Come unto me, all ye that labour and are heavy laden, and I will give you rest. Take my yoke upon you, and learn of me; for I am meek and lowly in heart: and ye shall find rest unto your souls. For my yoke is easy, and my burden is light.

Matthew 16:24-25: Then said Jesus unto his disciples, If any man will come after me, let him deny himself, and take up

his cross, and follow me. For whosoever
will save his life shall lose it: and
whosoever will lose his life for my sake
shall find it.

Envy & Jealousy

Envy and jealousy, while similar, are not
the same. Both are expressions of
covetousness, and both are directly
linked to murder. A person who is
jealous of you does not necessarily want
to be you, but they want what you have.
They may be jealous of the material
things you have, the lifestyle you live or
the relationships you have. A person
who is envious of you wants to be you or
to be like you. They have already written
off their own lives as worthless and are
so focused and obsessed with your life
that they don't necessarily covet the
things you have, they covet the life you
have. A person who is envious of you
does not necessarily want your lifestyle.
They may love the way you look and the
way you present yourself and covet that

for themselves. They may like your
personality or how others respond to
you. A person who envies you or is
jealous of you is a person who could
easily kill you. You'll notice that in most
of the stories of jealousy or envy in the
Bible, murder came on the scene. Cain
was jealous of Abel's relationship with
GOD, so he killed him. Saul was jealous
of David's relationship with GOD and the
anointing on David's life, so he tried to
kill him. Joseph's brothers were jealous
of Joseph's relationship with their
father, Jacob, so they plotted to kill him,
and eventually sold him off into slavery.
Of course, we know that Lucifer envied
GOD and wanted to be HIM. The most
shocking case of envy was found in
Genesis and occurred when Lucifer
tempted Eve. He told her she could be
as a god; she could be like GOD, thus
devaluing who she was and causing her
to covet the very life of GOD. When Eve
bit into the fruit, she disobeyed GOD,
causing her to come from under the

covering of GOD. Because she was uncovered, she realized she was exposed (naked). When she was covered by GOD, she was not aware of the fact that she was naked.

James 4:2: Ye lust, and have not: ye kill, and desire to have, and cannot obtain: ye fight and war, yet ye have not, because ye ask not.

Romans 1:29-31: Being filled with all unrighteousness, fornication, wickedness, covetousness, maliciousness; full of envy, murder, debate, deceit, malignity; whisperers, Backbiters, haters of God, despiteful, proud, boasters, inventors of evil things, disobedient to parents, Without understanding, covenantbreakers, without natural affection, implacable, unmerciful.

Galatians 5:21: Envyings, murders, drunkenness, revellings, and such like: of the which I tell you before, as I have also told you in time past, that they which do such things shall not inherit the kingdom of God.

Selfish Ambition

Selfish ambition, otherwise known as vain glory, means to be totally and unequivocally unlike GOD. GOD is not selfish by any means. Selfish ambition is to set one's self up as one's own god. It is to become an idol to yourself and to seek the glory of GOD for yourself. To be selfish is to be almost identical to Satan. Any person who exalts self is a person who has evicted GOD from their hearts. GOD is love, and without love, there's nothing else to do but hate. A person who is selfish is everything that GOD is not. They are inconsiderate, hateful, indifferent and unmerciful.

Philippians 2:3: Let nothing be done through strife or vainglory; but in lowliness of mind let each esteem other better than themselves.

Galatians 5:26: Let us not be desirous of vain glory, provoking one another, envying one another.

1 Corinthians 13:4-7: Charity suffereth long, and is kind; charity envieth not; charity vaunteth not itself, is not puffed up, Doth not behave itself unseemly, seeketh not her own, is not easily provoked, thinketh no evil; Rejoiceth not in iniquity, but rejoiceth in the truth; Beareth all things, believeth all things, hopeth all things, endureth all things.

Lack of Knowledge & Understanding

GOD tells us to seek both knowledge and understanding, along with wisdom. Without knowledge or understanding, however, one cannot acquire wisdom.

Have you ever suffered through a break-up or a betrayal? To be betrayed means that something happened which exposed that a person you've trusted has proven themselves to be unworthy of your trust. This means that GOD allows knowledge to come to the forefront so you can see what or who you have allowed in your heart. GOD told us to guard our hearts, for out of them flow the issues of life. Anytime we do not guard our hearts, however, we expose our hearts. It's like having an unlocked front door while living in a high crime area. We're living in perilous times, and we must guard our hearts now more than ever. Just as a thief would break into your unlocked home and steal your valuables, the thief (Satan) can break into your heart (if it's unguarded) and steal your joy. He also steals any Word that is not rooted in your heart. Anytime we've been hurt, we have to deal with the obvious things that have happened, and we tend to focus on those things that we can see. Focusing too much on the obvious will only cause you to hurt, marinate in your pain and hate the person who's caused you that pain. But there's another layer to everything that reveals itself in the earth realm, and it is usually found in the spirit realm. Remember, the war is not against flesh and blood, but against powers, principalities and the rulers of this dark world.

Any and every relationship you have is either GOD-rooted or soulish in nature. Anytime a believer enters a soulish union, be it a friendship or relationship, GOD turns on the light of knowledge so the believer can see where he or she is and who he or she is with. In other words, GOD gives us revelation knowledge, and when we get the chance to see what GOD sees, it often breaks our hearts. That's because whatever or whomever is hurting us has gotten into our hearts, and the truth comes to serve them their eviction notices.
From there, we are given a choice: Continue in the truth and be free or return to our Egypts (lands of bondage). If we choose to remain free, repent and turn back to GOD, GOD then gives us understanding of what we've been through. HE shows us layer upon layer over time, so we can go deeper and deeper into understanding until we

reach wisdom.

But when we refuse knowledge and understanding, we are in the same choosing to stay in rebellion. If we stay in rebellion, we will continue to endure the pains of having the wrong person in our hearts or being in the wrong place. This hurt alone is enough to cause a person to spiral into hatred.

Conclusion

Anytime we go into sin, we begin to pick up layers and layers of lies, hurts and soul ties. Oftentimes, our plans aren't to sin against GOD, but we think we can flirt with sin without it flirting back with us. Every time we reach a new layer of sin, we earn a new layer of pain. When GOD begins to reveal the truth to us, HE causes revelation to give us knowledge of each lie, each betrayal and each reality until we renounce that particular sin, and then HE begins shedding light on the next layer. This means that the deeper we go into sin, the more pain we will endure as the truth breaks the outer shells of our hearts on its journey to the innermost depths of our hearts. As each layer of lies is peeled back, we have to sit still and endure the pain. Knowledge is the surgeon that cuts into our hearts, but understanding is the stitches that help us to begin healing.

The Lesson

While still a babe in CHRIST, I met my
first husband. I'd left the club scene by
then, but I still had that old mindset, and
it was evident in the way I dressed and
the people I hung out with. We ended up
living together for two years before
getting legally married.

After we were married, I felt so much
better. I was no longer fornicating, so
my next focus was getting him to the
LORD. That's how a babe in CHRIST
thinks. I thought that I could take him
to church with me and that he'd share in
my convictions, but of course, this didn't
happen. The relationship was a
tumultuous one, and one where there
was a lot of fighting....just like the home
I'd grown up in. But the first lick didn't
come from him; it came from me. He'd

crossed the line one day by saying
something inappropriate to a cousin of
mine, and I'd hauled off and hit him as
hard as I could. At that time, I thought it
was okay to hit a man, and that he
wasn't supposed to hit me back. That
day, I was delivered from that mindset,
and even though I stopped passing the
first lick when we fought, the fighting
continued to escalate. I didn't think it
was abuse at that time because I fought
back on many occasions. I thought we
were just fighting, but he happened to be
the stronger one so the fights would end
when he'd pin me to the floor or up
against the wall with his hands around
my neck.

The years continued to pass, and what I
saw as fighting continued to escalate
into something far worse. It all started
with an affair he'd had with a woman
who was sixteen years older than the
both of us. The woman called my house
anytime I was away from home. It wasn't

long before she began to harass and stalk me.

On one particular day, my husband and I were in our bedroom when we heard the sounds of a horn being held in front of our house. We both ran towards the door, and to our surprise, his mistress was parked in our driveway holding her horn. When she saw us, she smiled at us, backed her vehicle up and drove away. She continued to come to our house from time-to-time and hold her horn until one of us would come to the door. Nevertheless, he continued to try and convince me that the woman was an old co-worker of his and that he'd never have an affair with a woman so old. I knew better, but I still wanted to believe him, so I'd argue with him, question him and tell him that we needed to go to the police about that woman. Of course, he didn't want the police involved, and he said he would handle her. According to him, she was mentally unstable and had probably had a crush on him without his knowledge.

The harassment continued to escalate until one day his mistress called and began to tell me that she'd slept with him in our bedroom. I knew she wasn't lying, but I also knew that he'd find a way to dismiss her accusations as lies. I wanted to force myself to face the truth, so I asked her to describe my bedroom to me, and she described it to perfection. She began to lay out how my furniture was positioned, and at the end of each sentence, she proudly and profanely referred to me as a "female dog." I didn't understand it at all. How could he cheat? And why was she cursing me out about a man I was married to? I hung up the phone with her and confronted him once again, but he continued to declare his innocence, stating that our bedroom blinds didn't fully cover the windows. He said she'd likely been peeping through our windows; nevertheless, he still insisted on not getting the police involved.

I continued to stay with him, enduring affairs, harassment from other women and being choked anytime a fight escalated. I found myself not only being hurt by what he was doing, but I was embarrassed. After all, we lived in a small city, and the news about our seemingly perfect marriage was spreading quickly. It wasn't long before my co-workers were standing in hurdles talking about my failing marriage. It wasn't long before people began calling me to ask about the older woman who was going around town telling anyone who'd listen that she was sleeping with my husband. I couldn't hurt privately because I felt like everyone knew things that I didn't know. This made the pain even more intense because I had nowhere to grieve or think. I couldn't hold my head up because I was afraid that someone could see the pain in my eyes, and I did not like people to see me hurt. I hated pity parties because to me, pain meant vulnerability, and I felt that being vulnerable would only expose me to people who'd see my pain as my weakness. I feared that they'd then try to use my weakness to hurt and exploit me, so I always tried to put on a strong front. I'd developed that fear as a child, and I'd carried it with me into my adult life.

Hatred began to tug at my heart once again. One day, I would say nice, little Christian things because that was who I was becoming, but the next day, I would be firing off profane words because that's what I'd became over the years.

Over time, things continued to get worse. He became colder towards me, and our fights became frequent. I lived in a state of confusion, not knowing whether he'd love me that day or if he'd kick off a fight so he could justify leaving home for the night. I didn't realize how close I was to having a nervous breakdown until I began to lose control of my hands from time-to-time. I would be working at my home computer or work computer, and all of a sudden, I would feel like I was being electrocuted. My arms would start to jerk around and I couldn't control them. These attacks would only last a few seconds, but it was long enough to get my attention.

One day, I did something I absolutely did not want to do: I broke down at work, and cried uncontrollably to one of my managers. A week or two later, I was breaking down in the office of another manager. The fighting kept getting worse, and he continued to become even more violent towards me. One particular night, he'd come home drunk in the middle of the night. He wasn't a drinker, but on that particular night, he'd gone out to a club and drunk some pretty hard liquor. I was upset that he'd come home so late, so I went and confronted him. I had a problem with my mouth back then, and I must admit that I could be brutal with my words when I was hurt. I stood in the doorway of the den, and I began to yell at him continuously. Suddenly, he got up and attacked me. This attack was nothing like any of the previous attacks. He was a lot more brutal than he'd been before. Before I knew it, I was being dragged down the hall towards our bedroom. When he got me to the bedroom, he threw me on the bed and began to scream to me that I'd better not leave the room. I won't lie and say I remember what threat he'd issued to me, but what I do remember is that I was afraid for my life because I didn't recognize him. He dumped out my purse and took my car keys and cell phone. After that, he snatched the house phone's cord out of the wall before throwing the phone to the floor and breaking it. Once he'd slammed the door shut, I sat on my bed in the darkness with my heart and mind racing.

It had all happened so fast, and I didn't know what to do. I knew he would be in the den, and the den was close to the front door, so there was no way I could run out the front door without him catching me. I knew I'd be taking a huge risk if I tried to run out the back door, but it was a risk I was willing to take.

I waited about ten minutes before I made my break for the back door. I wanted to get to a phone to call the police because he'd gone too far. Not only had he attacked me, but he had taken my possessions and was holding me against my will.

As I swung the back door open, I could hear him screaming my name. I only hoped he wouldn't go out the front door and intercept me, and he didn't. I think he went to the back room first, but I hadn't been running long before I heard our car crank up. I was overtaken with fear; nevertheless, I put all of my energy into that run. But that run wasn't a good one. As hard as I tried, I could not run fast; plus, it didn't help that I was wearing high-heeled boots. As I heard the vehicle approaching me, I realized I only had one choice to escape. I had to cut across someone's yard and head towards their backyard. I knew he wouldn't abandon the car to chase me all the way around the back of someone's house. After all, I'd had a similar situation happen to me with an ex-boyfriend some years back and common sense told me to cut yards when running from a moving vehicle.

Somehow, I ended up in the middle of the highway, not caring that vehicles were heading my way. I tried to stop a woman driving an SUV to ask for help, but she drove around me and kept going. Just as my feet touched the pavement on the other side of the highway, I heard the screeching sounds of tires. I looked up and saw that he'd pulled off the road just a few feet behind me. I took off running across another yard, and he jumped back into the vehicle. I began banging on the back door of someone's house, but understandably, no one came to answer the door. As I ran around that house, I noticed he'd pulled up in front of the house and was headed my way, so I ran back across the highway. Once I was on the other side of the highway, I began running through backyards until I saw a storage shed. I hid in the storage shed, trying to muffle the sounds of my cries. He was drunk, and I'd never seen him behave like that before. Sure, he'd been violent, but it had never been like that. That was the very first time I feared for my life.

For over an hour, I hid in storage sheds and behind houses. Here I was, a woman who'd never done drugs in her entire life, and I was running behind houses and hiding in sheds. I kept covering my mouth to muffle the sounds of my cries and my heavy breathing. I couldn't believe it had gone that far. I felt so low at that point.

As I looked towards the highway, I could see him driving slowly in our vehicle looking for me. Each time he'd get out of my sight, I'd run behind another house. I was trying to get closer to my own house, hoping that I could find my cell phone and call the police. After about an hour of hiding, I got tired of running from him, so I walked onto the pavement of a street not far from our house. I was ready to fight back or give up; I didn't care. I was just tired. Just as I was walking, I noticed a police car driving up behind me. As the car drove past me, I began to wave my hands and scream for them. Suddenly, they stopped and backed their vehicle up. There were two officers in the vehicle, and just as I started to tell my story to them, one of the officers interrupted and asked, "Are you Tiffany?" When I confirmed my identity with him, he told me that my husband had called the police and said he was worried about me. He told the officers that he'd come home drunk, and I'd started verbally attacking him. He said we'd gotten into a physical altercation, and I'd run out of the house. He told the cops that he'd chased me to try and bring me back home because it was the middle of the night and he was worried about me. I began crying and laughing at the same time as I told the officers the real story, but the officers had already been sold on his version of the story. They told me that he seemed genuinely concerned for me; he'd just had too much to drink, and after that, they offered to drive me back to my house to get my possessions from him.

When we got back to my house, my husband was home, and I began to tell my version of the story once again to the officers. I wanted so much for them to believe me. I wanted to have my husband arrested because he'd taken the abuse to a whole new level.

Nevertheless, the officers were unmoved. They told us that we both needed to just separate for the night so we could calm down. They said that one of us had to leave the house. Before I could say anything, my husband yelled to the officers that he was too drunk to drive and therefore, couldn't go anywhere. I volunteered to leave because I didn't feel safe in that house. Also, leaving meant I'd get back the keys to the car. When the officers had initially asked him for the keys, he'd refused to give them to me, saying the car was "our car," and the police responded by telling me they couldn't force him to give me the keys. Now that he was admitting to being drunk once again, I knew that this was the only opportunity I had to get those keys. I said to the officers, "I'll leave, but I need the keys to the car. He took my car keys from me." That's when my husband said to the officers that he wasn't giving me those keys. The officer then issued a threat to him, warning him that if he did not give the keys to me, he'd be arrested. Finally, he got up and brought me my keys and my cell phone.

I called a friend of mine who lived in a nearby town. It was about four in the morning, and I didn't know where to go. She didn't answer her phone, but I continued to drive towards her house. I felt like I was having an out-of-body experience. I cried and prayed as I drove down the dark roads that led to my friend's house. When I finally arrived, I began knocking on her door until she finally answered. When she heard my voice, she opened the door and I stood there with tears in my eyes and my voice cracking. I tried to tell her what happened, but at first, I couldn't muster out the words. When I finally finished the story, she began to do as I suspected she'd do. She began to yell at me, telling me that I needed to leave my husband.

Her father had been abusive to her mother and had taken her mother's life. I could hear her pleas for me to leave, but I could not fathom going back and living with my siblings. To me, it was no better than where I was. I feared staying and I feared leaving. I felt like I had no place to go, so the next day, I went back.

A few more years would pass before I got the strength to let go. For the time that I'd held on, I'd endured more affairs and more abuse, but the breaking point came when the LORD gave me a dream about my husband. In that dream, I'd saw him having sex with a woman, and I'd looked up to an uncle of mine who was standing next to me and said, "She's pregnant now. There's no way she's not pregnant." When my husband came home, I told him about the dream, and he finally admitted to having an affair and possibly impregnating another woman. I was sick with grief. I'd just suffered through my second miscarriage and hadn't fully recovered from that yet.

Even after his admittance to having impregnated someone else, I still stuck around for another year because he'd begged me to stay, promising he would be a better husband. I felt stupid, but I also loved him and kept replaying my promise to him in my mind. When we'd first met, he'd told me that everyone he loves leaves him, and I'd promised to stick around no matter how bad things would get. I didn't know at that time that his speech was one that abusers commonly give their would-be victims. I didn't know that those words were pretty much a verbal contract I was signing, committing to staying with him despite all he'd take me through. Like most abusers, he knew he'd hurt me. He just needed to know I'd stick around after he did.

A year later, he finally left to be with another woman. I was hurt, but relieved at the same time. I knew that the monster he'd been with me was the monster he'd be with her, so I couldn't be jealous of the two of them. I was only hurt that I was losing someone I loved. I cried, I prayed and I asked the LORD to put forgiveness in my heart for him and the mistress. I didn't want to hate them. I didn't want to even be angry with them. I just wanted to move on with my life because I was getting closer to GOD, and I wanted HIM to be pleased with my life. I didn't want to continue having a life where police officers were having to come to my home to intervene anytime our arguments turned into physical fights. I didn't want to be choked, slammed to the floor, or hit anymore. The last year of our marriage was when he'd upgraded his abuse to striking me. I didn't want to continue being the woman everyone whispered about. I wanted to get my life back and rebuild it. I wanted to have a normal life, a normal marriage and more than anything, I wanted GOD to be proud of me.

How did GOD bring me to forgive my ex husband? HE took me on a journey; a journey where I saw how imperfect I was too. I'd hurt people in my life. I'd played the role of the other woman before, and in an attempt to get revenge, I'd had a month-long affair after I discovered my ex had gotten another woman pregnant. Of course, he didn't know about that affair because I knew his response would have probably landed him with a life sentence in prison.

I was far from perfect. GOD showed me that I was never supposed to marry that man in the first place. I'd chosen him, and both of us were not ready to be married to anyone. Sure, I'd been a much greater wife to him than he was a husband to me, but that did not excuse the fact that I was a flawed human being who wasn't marriage-ready. Additionally, GOD showed me that I had wronged my ex by marrying him in the first place because I married him hoping I could change him. That was wrong on my part because I hadn't given him the same freedom that GOD had given me, and that's the ability to want change before attempting to change.

Oftentimes, we are so unfair to GOD. We go against HIS will for us, and then we complain when we see the fruit of our ways. As human beings, we often think we can change GOD'S mind by marrying who we want, when GOD told us that we have to be transformed by the renewing of our minds. HE also told us in HIS WORD that HE is not a man that HE should repent; neither is HE the son of man that HE should change HIS mind. It doesn't matter what you say to GOD, HE is not going to change HIS mind about that man or woman you've chosen for yourself. The only thing that changes when you marry or enter into a relationship with someone who is not in HIS will for you is the amount of time it'll take you to reach the blessings HE has for you. Anytime we go off course, our flights to elevation in HIM are delayed.

Anytime I come across a woman who badmouths her ex and blames him for being who he is, I have to remind her that he was who he is when she met him. The error was already in him for being that way, but the greater error was in her because she thought she could change a man who was refusing to change for GOD. Know this: Each situation you endure is designed to be a lesson to you, but if you don't learn the lesson, pass the test and move on, you'll end up going back through that lesson again until you finally grow up or give in.

Retaking the Lesson

By the time I met my second husband, I was more versed in the Bible. I'd actually grown closer to GOD during my first marriage, and I felt that I was ready to be a wife. I'd seen myself as a wife, and I was pretty proud of myself, so I didn't hesitate to accept my second husband's proposal. To me, he seemed like a better fit because he said he knew what he wanted. He wanted to be married and have a family. He had no children, he was just about to graduate from college, and he promised to be a faithful man. He wasn't in church or in the WORD, but again, I thought I could change that with my love.

Over the course of our marriage, I didn't witness too many problems with other women, even though I had my suspicions. He was an African man, so I attributed a lot of his bad choices to culture. I would often remind him that I was American and he should not communicate with his ex-girlfriends or go out randomly giving his number away to other women. It goes without saying that he saw my requests as attempts to control him. After all, in his culture, the women didn't question the men. You were to just be happy to have a man, and this mindset didn't fly well with me. Needless to say, we had our fair share of arguments. By the time I'd met and married him, I had been delivered from hatred for the most part. I'd forgiven everyone from my past, and I was rooted in the WORD of GOD; nevertheless, I didn't have enough WORD in me to understand that I was still too young spiritually to be married. But over the course of our marriage, I was exposed to hatred to the highest power.

My husband had a sister who constantly

launched attacks against me and our marriage. I became angrier and angrier with him for not standing up for me or for our marriage. Instead, he would often stand against me and tell me that I needed to just submit to his sister, and that just wasn't going to happen. I couldn't have submitted to her if I tried. It just isn't in me to bow down to anyone but GOD.

One day, she (my husband's sister) called my husband and told him that one of her female friends was coming into town, and she'd given the woman permission to stay at our house while she visited. Of course, I said no to this, and this started an argument between my husband and I that went on for weeks. There was no doubt about it. I was battling against a Jezebel spirit, and Jezebel had determined that I either needed to submit to her authority or lose my husband. I chose the latter.

There I was, married for the second time and in a fight for my marriage. My husband's sister had never been married, and she did not want to understand that she was not supposed to interfere in our marriage, or anyone else's marriage for that matter. At the same time, my husband was Cameroonian and was brought up to believe that his family came before his wife. Because of this, the meddling in-law mercilessly attacked our marriage with words, accusations, demands; you name it. I would argue with him because he did nothing to stop the intrusion in our marriage. He would take her advice time and time again, and this brought about many contentious battles in our home; a battle that would go on for years to come. After a while, I knew her voice, even though I'd stopped talking with her years ago. I knew when my husband was speaking from his heart, as opposed to when he was repeating her words. I knew his voice from her voice, and I began to grow weary of her intrusions. I also began to grow spiteful of the man I'd married because I did not understand why he would allow a godless woman who'd never been married to tell him how to handle, or better yet, mishandle me.

Because I'd learned to identify her voice, and she was calling him daily, I began to notice her daily presence in my home, even though physically she was states away. I started to notice that most of our arguments had her name in it because she would involve herself one way or another. Slowly, I began to despise her, and then one day, I said it. I wished her dead. I wanted to hear the news that she'd been killed somehow, somewhere. I was so tired of her that I felt the only solution to my problem was if she'd just drop dead. After voicing those words, I went away and attempted to repent to GOD. How could I say such a wicked thing? How could I want such a wicked thing?

As time went on, I found myself saying it and actually wishing for it again and again. I wanted to get the news that she was no longer in the realm of the earth because she interfered in everyone's marriage. She had brought so much misery to people, and I felt the only salvation for my marriage would be if she would just die. Every time I said or thought those words, I would go back and attempt to repent to GOD. Little did I know that I was not truly repenting; I was simply apologizing. I didn't take the time out to consider that out of the abundance of the heart, the mouth speaks. How could I be a Christian woman and wish someone dead? It's simple: I'd begun to hate her. After so many years of meddling and calling back-to-back, I'd had it with her. And that's when I went to the LORD for answers, and HE explained to me that it wasn't so much my words as it was the content of my heart. My words only reflected what I wanted, even though I'd silently kept those desires hidden away in my heart. I tried to hide those desires from myself. I tried to hide those desires from the LORD; nevertheless, they were still there. I'd fought against them and failed again and again. All it took to set me off was to hear another thing she'd said about me or advised my husband to do against me, and I was off somewhere spearheading her name with my words. Soon, I became unknowingly obsessed with her name because it was a name I heard daily. At the same time, my husband would make frequent trips to visit his sister, but I wasn't welcome to come because we didn't get along. Soon, he began to travel about eight times a year to different states and countries. When he traveled for his job, he had a legitimate excuse about not wanting me to come. He said it was a business trip, and none of his colleagues were bringing their wives. But we argued whenever he took trips to visit his sister because I didn't understand why I couldn't travel with him and the two of us just get a hotel room. Anytime he went to visit his sister, even if the trip was not supposed to be for her, he'd tell me that I couldn't come, and if I did, we'd be staying at her house. Nevertheless, he'd often tell me that she wanted to come to Florida to visit us, and when I said she wasn't welcome in our home, he'd get upset with me. Needless to say, she never came to our home because I was strongly against it. I became angrier and angrier because the message I began to understand was that it was okay for her to say I wasn't welcome at her home, but it wasn't okay for me to have those same rules.

On one particular trip to Georgia, I'd told my husband that his sister was going to ask to speak with me because he'd be on her turf yet again. By that time, I knew her ways, and I knew that she felt empowered anytime he was there with her. She felt like his visits were great opportunities for her to show me that he was her property. She wanted to use these opportunities to try to get me to do as her brother had done: submit to her. The whole issue between the two of us was that she controlled everyone in her family, including my husband, but I refused to be controlled. I knew that submission was only to be given to GOD and to my husband, but not some wicked woman who felt like I had to serve her in order to have her brother. She would often say to my husband that her problem with me was that I didn't listen to her. She said if I'd only listen, she would back off. When questioned as to what she meant by "listen," she said I didn't do what she said to do; I didn't take her advice.

Once my husband was at her house, he called me later that day. While we were talking, she came into the room and

asked him who he was speaking with.
He told her that he was talking to me, so
she asked to speak with me, but he
declined. After that, I could hear her
cursing and screaming all kinds of
profanities at me. She said she was tired
of me and that I'd been with my husband
three years and still hadn't given him a
child yet. She then said that the reason I
hadn't become pregnant was because
she'd cursed me. Of course, I laughed at
the idea. No one can curse what GOD
has blessed, and being that she is from a
small village in Cameroon, Africa, I
wasn't the least bit surprised when she
announced that she'd been attempting
witchcraft against me. She hadn't
learned, however, that witchcraft does
not work on a child of GOD. This did
confirm to me what I'd said to my
husband all along. I'd said that his
sister practiced witchcraft, and he'd
always laughed at the idea. After all,
he'd known her all of his life, and he
couldn't imagine her being a witch.

Even though she was screaming
obscenities at me, I remained calm.
That's how I knew GOD was in control. I
didn't feel the need to lash out or
threaten her. Instead, I laughed and told
my husband to call me back when he
had some alone time.

Over the next few years, her charades
continued. Some of my husband's
family members ended up getting
involved because she was obsessed with
me and my marriage, and she couldn't
stop talking about me. Again, the issue
was that she was accustomed to
controlling my husband but I would not
submit to her. She had a reputation in
her family for being the loud, controlling
and obnoxious relative with no tact, but
that didn't go well with me.

Once my husband's family members got
involved, they told her to go and find
herself a husband and to stop interfering
in my marriage. My husband's mother

forbade him from speaking with his sister any more than once a week because at that point, she was calling him several times a day, and I was ready to call it quits. For a while, he took his mother's advice and seemed to be sincerely sorry because his mother warned him that his sister had always been a problem wherever she went. Suddenly, our marriage felt real. We started holding hands more, we started kissing more, and he appeared to be more attentive. He apologized for allowing his sister to repeatedly attack me with her words and wicked suggestions. The heartbreak in his eyes and the sincerity of his voice made me believe that our marriage was taking a turn for the better. Nevertheless, this renewed spark was burned out only after a couple of months, when he'd began to revisit his old behaviors with his sister. His calls to her began to escalate more and more, and before I knew it, he'd become distant again. When I brought his behavior to his attention, even reminding him that his own mother said that his sister had always been a problem and he shouldn't talk with her so often, he snapped back with, "My mother is old. She doesn't understand. You and my sister will just have to find some way to get along."

Our marriage continued to go downhill as their communications escalated. I continued to find out secrets my husband had been hiding from me. I found out he had a secret bank account, he had a secret mailbox at the post office, he had been sending money to his family members without my knowledge, and he was calling his sister every day on his lunch break, even though he'd never called home to check on me.

Finally, the marriage gave way, and my husband filed for a divorce. A great part of me was relieved because I'd been so worn down over the years. I was tired of feeling like a second-class citizen to my own marriage.

The night he left was a good night for me. He'd come home and gotten upset with me because I'd thrown away something he'd recently brought back from Africa. It was in a small black bag and it was obviously decomposing, whatever it was. I'd complained about a horrible smell emitting from something in our apartment for the entire week that he'd been back home, but he continued to dismiss it as nothing. I couldn't take the smell, however, so I continued to search our residence for the source of the smell.

That particular week, the LORD had been giving me a lot of dreams. In one dream, there were two men and a woman, and they'd kidnapped me. The woman was extremely wicked, and she was the one who called the shots. One of the men was obviously her lover. He was aggressive and controlling, but he submitted to her. The other guy was very passive, almost as if he were her son.

In the dream, they'd taken me to their house, and I was placed in the passive guy's bedroom. It was obvious that I would be his property. I was afraid, so I didn't open my mouth to say much. Suddenly the wicked woman's lover came into the room and threw me on the bed. He said for me to take off my clothes. I was terrified because I knew he was "her" lover, and she was already a raging force to deal with. I didn't want her to get even angrier because her lover was coming after me. Just as I was sitting on the bed, the door opened, and she called his name. I thought she'd be angry, but she said to him that when he finished with me, to come and see her. He agreed, but I don't recall anything happening.
Suddenly, the dream took a turn for the

better. I heard noises, and then, somehow, I could see something come over her as she screamed in agony. I remember hearing I was being rescued, and then I woke up.

A few days later, I dreamed I was sitting on a bed and wearing a beautiful wedding gown. I couldn't see the man I was about to marry, but I was happy. I was in a room with a woman who was doing my hair and makeup. In the dream, I was worried about how I looked, so the woman who was beautifying me turned the mirror to me and I was taken aback by how beautiful I was. My hair was perfect, my gown was perfect, my makeup was perfect, and I was happy. Suddenly, I heard a noise in the hallway, so I stood up and went to the door. As I peeped out into the hall, I saw three wicked characters. They were all teenagers. Two of them were boys and one was a girl. As they passed by the room, they looked at me, and continued to look back at me, but I had an understanding that they could not enter that room, and I dared not leave it.

I began to understand that the LORD was telling me that I'd been rescued and that the people (and their tormenting demons) would no longer be able to torment me or have access to me. I was in a different place, and the place I was in was a room that they could not enter. The two men represented the two personalities of my husband. One represented the evil force that was driving him. The meek character represented who he really was underneath. The meek character was the person I'd grown to know and love.

I continued to look for the source of the smell with vigor each day, because it got worse each day. Finally, one day I woke up and heard the LORD tell me to get up and anoint the room my husband had been sleeping in. Every since he'd come back from Africa, I just could not bring myself to sleep in the same room as him because I could tell he was changed, and not in a good way. He was at work, and the LORD laid it upon my heart to search one of the bags he'd brought back from his trip to Africa. In that bag, I found a small bottle of olive oil. I heard the LORD tell me to throw that olive oil away. I took it outside and tossed it in the huge public trash bin sitting in front of our apartment. Once I'd gone back into my apartment, the smell had gotten so intense that I could barely stand breathing. I went into the kitchen once again, and I began to sniff around. I opened the refrigerator and then the freezer, but the smell wasn't coming from the fridge. I began to follow the source of the smell, and I realized it was rising up in my nose; meaning, it was coming from down below. I got on my knees and opened the stove, and the smell was even more intense. There was nothing in the stove, but then I noticed a cabinet next to the stove. I opened that cabinet, and in there, I found a black bag full of items that were wrapped up in brown paper bags and taped shut. My husband had brought these items back from Africa.

When I opened the black bag, the smell almost knocked me over. It was so putrid that I felt like gagging. Then I noticed movement. As I stared into the bag, I suddenly saw maggots moving around whatever was wrapped in one of the brown bags. I was shocked and angry. I took the bag outside and placed it in the trash next to our apartment door. We had valet trash collection, so they'd normally pick up our trash from by the door. After placing the black bag in the trash, I text messaged my husband and told him that I'd found the source of the smell, and it was obviously decomposing flesh of some sort because it had maggots. He told me to leave the bag in front of our apartment, and he said he'd check it out when he came home.

I wasn't at peace about what I'd just witnessed. It was all surreal to me. Was this an attempt to perform witchcraft? I knew that it more than likely was, and the thought made me even angrier. Pacing back and forth, I called a friend of mine and told her what I'd just witnessed. She said to me, "Tiffany, you know that when he (your husband) gets home, he's going to bring that bag back into the house. You should have thrown it in the big trash bin and not said a word, because now, y'all are gonna fight when he tries to bring it back in. GOD showed you that bag for a reason." I thought about it, and I knew she was right, so I went back out and took a picture of the content of the bag. I wanted a picture to prove to my husband that maggots were really in the bag. I then took the bag to the large community trash bin and tossed it as far back as I could.

When I got back into my apartment, the smell had begun to subside. I began to speak and bind every devil, power and principality, and I commanded the angels of GOD to arrest every ungodly spirit and cast it into the pit until the Day of Judgment. I felt a peace beginning to break through the otherwise thick atmosphere. I continued to go through my apartment and wage war against the enemy. I declared that the enemy could not step foot into my apartment anymore, and if he did, he'd be immediately arrested by the angels of GOD. With every declaration, I felt a breaking and a calm.

Later that evening, my husband arrived home, and I stood up as he unlocked the door. He attempted to put one foot in our apartment, and then he withdrew that foot back out. Immediately, his eyes seemed darker and his voice became heavier and angrier. He looked in the trash next to my door and noticed the bag wasn't in the trash. With his voice raised, he asked me where the bag was, and I told him I'd thrown it away in the community bin. With fury in his eyes, he began to yell at me and demand I tell him where the bag was. I continued to repeat that I'd thrown it away and that it wasn't recoverable. He suddenly stepped into the apartment and began to tell me that I was a horrible wife and how much he didn't want me. I sat at my computer, and my flesh began to wake up. I stood up and told him that if he'd resorted to practicing witchcraft, he should just leave. He continued his verbal lashing and told me that he didn't want me and he was leaving me. The LORD said to me to just be quiet and sit down. HE told me not to say a word. HE then gave me peace in the midst of it all. As my husband hurriedly packed his bags and took them to his car, I sat still at my computer, continuing to ignore my husband's rants. I turned my phone's voice recorder on to record some of the harsh things he was saying, but truthfully, I knew I wasn't battling with him; I was battling with a spirit. It took him less than an hour to pack his bags, and before he left, he turned and looked at me, and then he said, "I'm moving out!" I nodded and said "okay," and he turned around and left.

After he left, I felt a peace that surpassed all understanding. I understood why I felt so happy and peaceful. I had been delivered from a marriage that was definitely not GOD'S will for me. Little did I know that there was an issue brewing in me that I had to be delivered from.

As the days and the weeks passed, the hurt began to set in. I began to cry more, and I revisited that last night again and again in my imaginations. I knew I'd handled the situation properly, but I did not recognize the force that came in wrapped in my husband's skin. I began

117

to revisit our marriage in my mind, and
the love I had for my husband started to
become an enemy to me. I didn't want to
love him, because loving him meant I
had to hurt, but I knew I couldn't stop. I
found myself getting angrier and angrier
with him, and then I remembered that he
was on the phone with some woman the
night he'd moved out. He'd placed her
on hold and let her listen to everything
that was going on and everything that
was being said. I started to consider the
obvious. He had likely been talking to
his sister the whole time.

I kept trying to throw myself into more
and more work so I wouldn't feel the
hurt that I knew would follow. The day
after my husband moved out, he'd sent
me an email with a form to remove his
name from the lease on our apartment.
Not long after that, he asked me to come
with him to remove my name from one of
his bank accounts. It was all becoming
more and more real, and it was

happening faster than I could mentally process. It was obvious; we were headed for divorce.

Even though I knew I was being delivered, I still felt as if I'd been robbed. I continued to peacefully communicate with him, and I went along with him to remove my name from his bank account and to remove his name from the lease on our apartment.

One day, the feelings had all begun to overwhelm me, and I found myself feeling more angry than I was hurt. I sat at my computer and tried to work, but the pain and the anger were too much for me. That's when I heard the LORD tell me to turn off my computer for 24 hours and to come and talk with HIM. I turned off my computer and cell phone. I then laid on the couch and began to cry with such an intensity that I knew I was at my breaking point. The LORD then told me to tell HIM how I felt about my

husband and his sister. I opened my
mouth and kept saying what I'd forced
myself to believe. At first, I said, "I
forgive them. They are evil, but I know
they'll be repaid. They only did what
they knew how to do."

The more I repeated those words, the
more GOD said to me, "Tell me how you
really feel." HE knew that I was hiding
hatred in my heart, even hiding it from
myself. I was trying to cover up that
hatred with nice little Christian words,
and I'd told myself that I'd forgiven my
soon-to-be ex-husband because I had
been being so nice to him. GOD
wouldn't let me stay in that hatred,
however. HE continued to ask me how I
felt about them until I broke.
I cried out, "Okay, I hate them and I wish
they were dead!" Those words shocked
me. I didn't know I was harboring
hatred, but pride had kept me from
visiting the real content of my heart.

I immediately began asking the LORD to take that hatred and unforgiveness from me. I told HIM the truth: I could not deliver myself. I needed to be free of that hatred once and for all. HE'D delivered me from hating my husband's sister once before, but those feelings had come back because I partly blamed her for my marriage failing. When my husband told me that his sister said if I had just listened to her, I could have kept my marriage, I had to fight all over again to not despise her. After all, I was dealing with a demonic spirit, not a person. Their battle wasn't against me; it was against the WORD in me.

After confessing that anger and hatred, GOD began to immediately deliver me. GOD explained to me that the enemy oftentimes doesn't attack us to bring us down. He attacks us so he can attach unforgiveness to us. The enemy knows he won't be successful in bringing down a believer who is in the LORD;

nevertheless, he knows that the believer is wrapped in flesh. If given the opportunity, he will attack us again and again, using the same people, until we grow to hate those people. In hating them, we stand on the wrong side of the war, fighting a war against love. I'd been duped. I'd been so focused on my husband's sister and all of her evils that I'd taken my eyes off of the spirit that was in operation within her. This war is not a war of flesh and blood; it's spiritual. Like Samson, I had been lying in the bed with someone who was exposing my weaknesses to the enemy. Like Samson, my weak spot was revealed, and the enemy captured me, then blinded me to the truth. I no longer saw people; I saw individuals I felt were worthy of nothing more than being living bulls-eyes for target practice. My eyes were blinded by hate, but love came in and opened them again.

As I submitted to GOD more, HE

continued to give me revelation of what I'd endured. Suddenly, I couldn't hate my soon-to-be ex-husband or his sister anymore. They'd done what they knew how to do. One day, my ex stopped by the apartment to pick up some mail that had come for him, and he began to apologize for everything that had transpired. He said to me, "I wasn't a man. I didn't protect you, and I'm sorry." We talked, and I felt a different kind of love for him. Not a romantic love, but a sisterly love. I began to weep for his soul, and I started to minister to him. We both cried and I asked him if I could pray with him before he left. He agreed, and I began to pray for him. After that, he began to tell me about the things he'd been witnessing, and we talked about his last night at the apartment. He wasn't aware that he'd brought olive oil back with him. When I told him, his eyes got bigger and I could tell he was worried. After that day, he and I continued to be friendly with one another. I continued and still continue to pray for him. The love I found in me for him had changed, and I began to witness the love GOD has for him. The thought of him going to hell hurt me more than anything, and I just couldn't sit still and let that happen. Even though we were going through a divorce, I still wanted to see him again in Heaven. I saw the meek and loving man underneath all the evil, and I knew that GOD loves that man.

Hatred often forms when we take our eyes off the truth, and we place our focus on the flesh and its operations. It's so easy to hate flesh because flesh has no inheritance. It is full of sin, and it opposes the Spirit of GOD. We can hate what we see, but that's why GOD tells us to walk by faith and not by sight. It's what we can't see that's oftentimes the culprit. Take that child, for example, who's been abused his whole life. He was abandoned by his dad, and his mother was unfit. He spent his life being shuffled around from his grandparents to his parents to other family members. He's never known stability; therefore, he grows up to become an unstable man. He was hurt at home and ridiculed at school. He becomes spiteful towards people, and engages in a life of crime. His crime happens to be a contact crime where he robs, beats and even rapes his victims. Now, when we see him, we see a monster who needs to be incarcerated for life or euthanized, but GOD sees something different. GOD sees a wounded soul who does not know how to empathize with others because he's never experienced anyone empathizing with him. We grew up, and even though our homes may not have been ideal, we knew empathy, we knew love, and we learned how to forgive through trial and error. After all, we had to live with our siblings; therefore, we had to learn to forgive them again and again. But this guy has never learned that. All he has ever known is heartache; therefore, heartache is what he serves. The prison system incarcerates him, and they call this rehabilitation, when in truth, it's simply a cage to keep him in. Should we free him to hurt someone else? Of course not. But what we should do is intervene in the lives of more children like him so they won't end up taking his path. After all, hurt people hurt people. His hatred stems from the fact that he's never gotten to know love.

Having lived with my ex-husband, and after having seen the good in him, I couldn't bring myself to live in hatred towards him. He's not a bad person. He's just a man who needs to find CHRIST and get delivered. What GOD wanted me to see is why HE loved him. I got a chance to witness the good in him to the point where I could not and cannot fathom the idea him going to hell. If I don't want him to go to hell after all he's done to me, just imagine how GOD feels about HIM. In reviewing all I'd been through with him, I came to realize that I could not blame his sister for the destruction of my marriage. She was just a willing pawn in Satan's schemes. Of course, my husband bore more of the blame because he'd allowed her to do the things she'd done, but I still don't blame him. Why not? I was dealing with a man who grew up in a country where witchcraft is just an ordinary part of life. He didn't kidnap me and force me to marry him. When I married him, I was in rebellion. I went against GOD and chose my own husband; therefore, the error was in me. As I continued to grow in GOD, it was inevitable that my marriage would end. After all, there were many times my husband could have chosen salvation, but like many unbelievers, he chose to continue in what he knew. When we'd met one another, both of us had secretly decided that we would change one another. I thought I could bring him away from Catholicism by showing him what Catholicism represented. He thought he could bring me away from Christianity by showing me what he believed Catholicism represented. We'd spent our marriage constantly trying to pull on each other, and as GOD continued to grow me up in HIM, I found my priorities continuing to change. I was growing in the LORD, so I had to stay focused on the ministry GOD entrusted me with, and had I been obedient and waited on GOD for the husband HE has for me, the two of us (my GOD-ordained husband and I) would be growing in CHRIST together. We'd be ministering together, and while growing in the LORD, we'd continue to grow closer to each other. In other words, it was my fault I'd gone through what I had. Think about it this way: Let's say you went out and married a crack addict. In your mind, you think you can change him, so you spend years throwing away pipes, calling the police on your husband, crying to your husband, crying out to GOD and looking for ways to reach your husband. One day, your husband meets another crack addict and decides he can't take your intrusive ways anymore. You are intruding upon his lifestyle. He likes doing crack. You're the only one (besides GOD) who has a problem with his habit, and if he doesn't care what GOD thinks, why is he going to care what you think? He leaves you for the crack addicted woman who prostitutes herself to feed her habit. But you are a successful business woman who looks far better than the weathered prostitute who's run off with your spouse, so you can't understand what's so special about her that he'd be willing to lose you. The answer is obvious. She's more like him than you are. That's the price of marrying the wrong man. Even when he's discovered you, he can never find you because GOD has hidden you in HIMSELF for your GOD-ordained husband. Why get upset with the man for being what he was when he met you?

The Hatred

The enemy is running a campaign to get hatred into the hearts of as many people as he can. He does this by using people who've been hurt to go out and hurt others, thus continuing the cycle of hurt. He knows that most of the people who are victimized will grow up to hurt someone else, and many of their victims will grow up to continue the cycles of hurt. My ex-husband's sister had been hurt a lot, and she'd allowed herself to become a willing conduit of pain. Satan wasn't as interested in bringing me down as he was in filling me up with hatred. He knew that I was helping other women to heal. I was pouring out into others, so he tried to contaminate my heart. Out of the heart flows the issues of life. By contaminating me, he'd cause me to become a polluted source that would infect anyone who'd dare open themselves up to me. That's why GOD continued to deal with me, even having me be silent at times so he could deal with my heart. Only when I poured out to HIM was HE able to pour into me, so I could let HIS WORD flow from me to HIS children. The assignment my ex's sister had was to get me into hatred, but every time I went there, the living GOD would bring me back. Every time I found myself hurt, the LORD would comfort me. Every time I found myself wishing for the worst, GOD would fill me with HIS best. I forgave my ex's sister when I came to understand that as wicked as she was, GOD still loved the woman underneath it all. To love someone is to pray for the deliverance of their soul, for CHRIST gave HIS life for the redemption of our souls. Sure, my ex's sister was one of the wickedest people I'd ever met in my life, but her attacks only brought me closer to GOD. Her attacks caused me to study warfare all the more, and to come to understand what demonic spirits are. Her attacks caused me to better understand the Jezebel spirit, just as I learned firsthand what an Ahab spirit was. I saw things I would never have believed I would see, but GOD was training me for warfare. I had to endure one-on-one training against a devil. I saw hatred in its purest form. I saw how souls submitted to the enemy. On one occasion, I'd gotten fed up with trying to get my husband to understand what a Jezebel spirit is and to stop allowing himself to become an Ahab. The LORD led me to open my husband's laptop and let him watch a forty-minute video detailing what that spirit was and how it operated. As he watched the video, his eyes got bigger and he kept saying, "Oh my gosh." After watching the video, he looked at me and said, "It's like that man (the narrator) knew my sister. My sister has that spirit." He was so taken aback by that video that he sent it to another relative and asked her to listen to it. Not long after that, he went to visit his sister, and when he'd come back, his words were different. Suddenly, when we spoke about the Jezebel spirit, he would repeat the same words over and over again as if he was reading from a script. It was surreal. He kept saying, "I was wrong. My sister does not have a Jezebel spirit." I was amazed, because before he'd left, he was passionately talking about that video for weeks, even begging his relative to watch it. But once he'd come back home, the passion was gone from his voice, and he wouldn't look at me as he disclaimed again and again, "I was wrong. My sister does not have a Jezebel spirit."

I had to come to grips with the fact that I was living with a man who needed some major deliverance. For years, I'd ignored the obvious, and for years, I'd made our fights all about his sister. I had been distracted, and the enemy had successfully thrown me off his trail. I'd finally learned my lesson, but I'd had to go through some pretty intense trials just to get it.

Hatred is made up of three things: lack

of knowledge, unforgiveness, and rebellion.

Lack of knowledge: To lack knowledge is like lacking water while in a desert. Anytime we lack knowledge, we continually place ourselves in situations and amongst people who hurt us. These people know pain; therefore, they will introduce their pain to us again and again until it becomes our pain. After all, they are attempting to relate to us. "Can two walk together, except they be agreed?" (Amos 3:3). Understand that when someone hurts you, it is oftentimes because they cannot understand you, but when you are hurting, they can relate to you. For example, let's talk about that meddling in-law who does everything in their power to destroy a marriage. Let's say that Felicia was married to Jacob, and Jacob's mother was interfering in their marriage. Jacob's mother does everything to destroy her son's marriage because Felicia won't follow her lead.

Felicia is too independent. Jacob's
mother introduces Jacob to other
women, and she speaks harshly to
Felicia. One day, Felicia is hurting and
goes to Jacob's mother to talk about the
affairs Jacob has been having. Suddenly,
his mother has a change of heart. She
now likes Felicia and attempts to console
her. She embraces her daughter-in-law,
and attempts to advise her. Now, she
harshly and angrily scolds Jacob for his
affairs. What just happened here? Did
Jacob's mother have a shred of love in
her? No. Jacob's mother is obviously a
woman who is full of hurt, hatred and
unforgiveness; therefore, she could not
relate to Felicia when Felicia was whole.
But now that Felicia is broken, she can
relate to her. Felicia is suddenly like a
daughter to her. Now, she's willing to go
against her son on Felicia's behalf, but
make no mistake about it, her sudden
change of heart has nothing to do with
loving Felicia. It has everything to do
with some unresolved issues that

Jacob's mother has in her own heart. People who are full of hate often see people as templates of the people who have hurt them. Now that Felicia is hurting, Jacob's mother can see herself in Felicia. Because of this, Jacob now becomes the template of the men who have hurt her. His mother will not encourage Felicia's healing. She will only comfort her and attempt to protect her from the monsters that have made her become the bitter creature she is today. She will take Felicia's youth and live vicariously through her. She will attempt to right her wrongs through Felicia. As long as Felicia is hurting, she will adore and spoil Felicia; nevertheless, if Felicia decides to come out of her pain, her mother-in-law will feel betrayed and may become more hateful towards her than she was beforehand. In this case, Felicia is undoubtedly dealing with a Jezebel spirit, and she will have to enter some SERIOUS warfare and fasting to come against that wicked principality. If

Felicia is not careful, her mother-in-law will invite her over for many discussions about men and how evil they are. She will plant a seed of hatred in her, and she will prune the love away from Felicia's heart, all the while watering the hatred within her.

Unforgiveness: GOD told us not to let the sun go down on our wrath. Why is this? That's because anything that's not dealt with immediately can and will eventually find its way into our hearts. It doesn't take long for a thought to become a heart issue. GOD told us to cast down imaginations and every high thing that exalts itself against the knowledge of GOD. When we don't cast it down, it has to be cast out. Unforgiveness is basically stored up wrath that has made its residency in our hearts. Vengeance belongs to GOD. All the same, the people who have offended and hurt us have probably already repented for what they've done. If you're walking around still accusing them of their sins against

you, you become a liar. How is that?
Once they repented, GOD cast their sins
into a sea of forgetfulness, and HE said
HE would remember them no more.
When you come along accusing them of
doing something that HE has tossed out
and forgotten about, you are the only
one who will be found guilty. You
become guilty of lying because the Blood
of JESUS has washed them clean and
declared them innocent. You become
guilty of vengeance. You become guilty
of hatred and malice. That's why it is
vital to your existence that you forgive
everyone who has hurt you. Remember,
a lot of the attacks Satan sent out
against you didn't come to bring you
down. Satan knew you'd still be
standing after the attack. Satan attacked
you because he was trying to get you to
open your heart to unforgiveness. That's
why the Bible tells us to guard our
hearts, for out of it flow the issues of
life. If hatred somehow gets into your
heart, then hatred will flow from your

life.

Rebellion: Even though many of us know
what GOD said, we rebel against HIS
WORD when we feel we have a better
idea. We are a people who love
immediate results, but the things of GOD
often require that we be patient. When
we refuse to wait, we step into rebellion.
Oftentimes, we want to see our enemies
brought down quickly, and even though
GOD has already judged them, HE still
extends grace to them. In other words,
HE gives them a grace period to repent
for what they've done, but if they do not
repent, HE then chastens or judges them
according to their works. If they do
repent, we must understand that they
are not the same creature who
committed the crime(s) against us. They
are all new again. True repentance isn't
saying that we are sorry; true repentance
is witnessed in a man's heart. It is him
confessing to GOD that he has done
wrong and is truly sorry for it, but it's
not his words that qualify him as

repentant; it is the direction of his heart. If and when he turns away from his wicked ways, and he acknowledges that he was wrong to GOD, only then is he forgiven for his sins.

How Hatred Reacts

Hatred is a poison of the heart. It consumes the person it possesses. Hatred is poison to the soul. It opposes GOD and HIS WORD, and it encourages the person it inhabits to seek redemption from the hurt that's driving them. Hatred stirs up wrath and unforgiveness. But there is something else that hatred stirs up; something that completely makes the person unlike GOD, and it's called selfishness.

If we've been hurt, we can't help but to pay attention to our wounds. If we've been betrayed, we can't help but notice what that betrayal did to us. The problem isn't noticing what the pain did; the problem lies in staying in what the pain did. Too many people park their hearts in pain and then complain that their lives aren't going anywhere.

To be selfish is to be totally unlike GOD. It is to walk in direct opposition of GOD and HIS will. This means that the person who is selfish becomes self-seeking. Their hearts, their thoughts and their plans are pointed at themselves, thus denying GOD the glory that is owed to HIM. GOD called us to unity, and HE wants us to love our neighbors as we love ourselves. This is to keep us from getting so wrapped up in ourselves that we become like his enemy, Satan. Let's reflect back to what Satan did to get himself kicked out of Heaven. Satan (Lucifer) was an angel in Heaven, and he led a revolt against the LORD. One third of the angels in Heaven fell with him. Lucifer's problem was that he became envious of GOD. He wanted to share in GOD'S glory, and of course, GOD does not share HIS glory or HIS throne. Lucifer boldly and foolishly thought he could overthrow GOD and take HIS place, and he was wrong. What happened to him? He became self-seeking. He wanted his own glory. Even though he had no needs, and he was in the presence of the Almighty GOD, he still wasn't satisfied. He became envious of GOD, and envy walks hand-in-hand with hatred. It is almost impossible for a person to envy you and not hate you.

When wrath sits in a person's heart for too long, it slowly simmers and becomes unforgiveness. When left to its own devices, unforgiveness slowly morphs into hatred. When someone allows wrath, unforgiveness and hatred to sit up in their hearts, they have no choice but to become selfish because every crime needs a victim. In their minds, they become the person who was wronged, and the person who wronged them becomes a moving target. For them, their life and their peace won't sit still until that target is no more. Now, many people who allow hatred to come into their hearts will not murder another human being, even though hatred is tied to murder; nevertheless, many will secretly wish for the death of their enemies. This is because when we feel victimized, we take the "good guy" role, and our movies don't end until the "bad guy" has been overcome.

Hatred distracts you from what you are supposed to be doing at any given time. GOD gives us seeds, and we have to water those seeds until the season of harvest is upon us. The enemy wants to distract us by causing us to consume the seeds, throw the seeds away, forget to sow the seeds, forget to water the seeds or forget to harvest the seeds. He even attempts to get us to abort the conception of any blessing due to be delivered in our lives. So he sends people our way; people who have been inhabited or oppressed by demonic spirits. The closer the person can get to us, the more damage they can do. GOD told us to guard our hearts, but Satan looks for any opening we may have in our hearts, and he looks for a void. If he finds the void, he offers to fill it, all the while using that opportunity to sneak into our hearts through whatever open doors we have in our lives. He desires to get someone on demonic assignment to create a soul tie with us, because a soul tie gives him in-house access to our hearts through whomever we have the soul tie with. That's why he tries to yoke up a believer with an unbeliever. He can't possess the believer, but hatred can because hatred has to be willed in.

Like love, hatred is not an emotion; it is a stronghold of the mind. Nevertheless, love is a Spirit. In order to hate someone, we have to meditate on what they've done to us. In other words, we become obsessed with them. Our minds are oftentimes distracted by thoughts of them and what they did to us. Our lives are oftentimes derailed by their choices.

What this indicates is that the person who is unleashing all of these distractions in our lives is clearly an intruder who should not be in our lives, or their seasons in our lives have expired.

It goes without saying that hatred will change how we view life and people. Not only does it affect our moods, hatred affects our health because the human body was not designed to hold hatred; it was designed for love. Hateful people are oftentimes challenged in their bodies by diseases because hatred will attack a person from the inside out. I remember shopping at the local Wal-Mart when a lady rolled by me on an automatic rolling cart. She almost hit me with the cart, and she was unapologetic. Her face showed that she was full to the brim with hatred. She didn't care who she hurt because she has been hurting for a long time. Hatred and unforgiveness are what likely caused her to have so many infirmities in her body. Now, this doesn't mean that everyone who can't walk or finds it hard to walk is full of hatred because that's not true. It simply means, in her case, that I saw what I believed to be the culprit, and this wasn't the first time that had happened. When I worked at a Wal-Mart in Mississippi, I'd seen that same situation many times. I'd seen people coming through the store who were obviously FULL of hatred. I was in the world then, but I could still identify the look of hatred on their faces. When they opened their mouths, they confirmed what I believed. Many of them had challenges in their bodies. Others had challenges in their thinking. They were mentally handicapped. Many people who are suffering from physical handicaps are not hateful, but most people that are hateful suffer from physical handicaps. That's what hatred does to a person. Hatred doesn't move in and bless the person it inhabits. Hatred is a poison that will slowly abuse the soul until it can no longer fight back. The enemy, on the other hand, will tell the person who hatred is inhabiting that to forgive the person who offended them is to release them. In order for them to get their overdue punishment, they need to hold them accountable for what they did, even if what they did was a half of a decade ago. What the enemy doesn't tell them is that they are not hurting the person they are angry with; they are actually opening themselves up to his poison and hurting themselves.

Hatred also keeps us from hearing the voice of the LORD. GOD is holy, and we can't approach HIM in an unholy way. GOD is love, and we can't approach HIM with hatred draped around our hearts. GOD is a forgiving GOD, and we can't approach HIM with unforgiveness dangling from our souls. So many people can't get their prayers to reach Heaven because they are trying to approach a holy GOD in an unholy way.

Matthew 5:23-24: Therefore if thou bring thy gift to the altar, and there rememberest that thy brother hath ought against thee; leave there thy gift before the altar, and go thy way; first be reconciled to thy brother, and then come and offer thy gift.

In Matthew 5:23-24, GOD is telling us not to approach HIM if there is a problem between us and our brothers and sisters in the LORD.

Hatred destroys marriages. How so? A person who has hatred in their hearts will oftentimes point that hatred at their spouse. After all, hatred lives in their hearts; therefore, it will flow from their lives, their words and their choices. They will just be hateful....period. A hateful person is a wrathful person. A hateful person is an unpredictable person. The spouse doesn't know which side of them they are coming home to on any given day.

149

Hatred puts our children at risk. If our children never witness forgiveness in us, they won't know how to access forgiveness when they've been hurt. At the same time, having hatred in one's heart is having strife in one's heart. Strife gives the devil a place, and if he can get in our hearts, he can get in our homes.

Ephesians 4:26-27: Be angry, and sin not: let not the sun go down upon your wrath: Neither give place to the devil.

Hatred causes us to magnify our own problems, and not the LORD. We must remember that we were created to worship the LORD in Spirit and in Truth. When hatred is in a man's heart, his mind has been compromised, and he can't worship GOD with his heart; he can only worship HIM with his mouth, and this is unacceptable to GOD.

Isaiah 29:13: Wherefore the Lord said, Forasmuch as this people draw near me with their mouth, and with their lips do honour me, but have removed their heart far from me, and their fear toward me is taught by the precept of men."

Hatred does many things to the human soul. If allowed in, it affects one's health, mind and lifestyle. It stands between the prayer and GOD, ensuring that their prayers don't reach Heaven.

Why Hate?

I remember that as a child, I tried to figure out this whole hate thing. I was around four or five years old, and I knew how to apologize when I'd done wrong. I remember standing outside of my grandparents' house one day looking down at the ground and saying, "Satan, why don't you just apologize to GOD for what you did?" I didn't understand that Satan cannot repent. Judgment has already been declared against him, but you can repent. There is only one act that you cannot and will not be forgiven for.

Matthew 12:31: Therefore I say unto you, All manner of sin and blasphemy shall be forgiven unto men: but the blasphemy against the Holy Spirit shall not be forgiven unto men.

Why hate what you do not understand? What you will discover is that the more you open up your mind to the knowledge around you, the happier you will be. Do you hate people of a different race or color? Try going to another country and being the foreigner there for a year or so. People who are traveled tend to be more open, sympathetic and loving than people who have not traveled, because we as humans tend to draw conclusions about a people based on what we've seen on television or what we've heard from others. Additionally, when we don't understand a thing, we fill in the blanks with what we perceive and what we believe, and oftentimes, our perception is our deception.

The marriage to my second husband did have some perks for me. I traveled to Germany a lot while with him, even staying there for six months with him. I'd even traveled to many European countries while with him, and I'd embraced a whole new outlook on life. I'd met so many people of different races, and I didn't realize how ignorant I was until I'd met them. One of the biggest misconceptions I had was in relation to African people. Of course, just like Americans, they have some wicked characters who live amongst them, but I've come to understand that they aren't all bad. All Africans aren't poor or running around naked. Being raised in a small city in Mississippi made it easier for me to relate to my husband because we found that southern upbringing was somewhat similar to African upbringing. At the same time, I realized that poverty looks the same everywhere you go. If you'll notice, the people in most of the places (if not all) that are poverty-stricken have some evil beliefs and practices. In Africa, voodoo and other forms of witchcraft are prevalent. Mississippi is one of the poorest states in the United States. When someone is poor in Mississippi, they are oftentimes very poor, and many poverty-stricken homes have a hint of witchcraft in them. Growing up, it was not uncommon for me to hear someone say they were going to cast a spell on a man to make him love them. I would often share stories with my husband of some of the foolish things I'd witnessed or stories I'd heard when growing up. When he saw many of the poor areas in my city, he would often say, "I'd rather go back to Africa than live in Mississippi. This place isn't too different from Africa."

Being with him taught me to understand that everyone has a story and that my story wasn't the worst one out there. I met African women who'd grown up in polygamist households where they'd been mistreated by their second and third moms. Their stories were horrible, and I couldn't imagine having lived through them. I met African women who'd grown up in homes where witchcraft was practiced. I've heard stories of how people would just go to a witch doctor (referred to as a herbalist by some Africans), and would pay him to kill someone they hated. According to these stories, the ones who were cursed would be walking one day and fall dead, and the doctors couldn't find anything wrong with them...except, of course, that they were dead. At the same time, I've heard some really good African stories. I've witnessed the similarities between African parents with African-American parents. I began to expand the walls of my heart to love a people who I could not relate to. I also began to understand why missionary work is VERY important in a lot of third-world countries.

People who hate others are people who need, of course, more of the WORD of GOD in them, and they need more exposure to the people they've come to hate. Most of the time, what manifests itself as hatred is often fear or intimidation. Believe it or not, many hate groups hate the very people they have built their lives on opposing. They not only fear these people, but they fear the potential of those groups to rise. Many gang members were brought up in homes that were filled with hatred, so hate is all they know. Having been broken at one point in my life, I can tell you what that brokenness does to people. It makes them walk around always on the offensive and always expecting the worst. When I'd been molested and hurt by men, I took up my war against a certain type of man. Hate groups take up their wars against a certain type of people. Getting to the root of the hatred in every individual person is the only effective way to usher them towards deliverance. Telling a man that he shouldn't hate his neighbor is ineffective if you don't introduce him to his neighbor. Hate groups and hateful people often feed on perception, and they are driven by a need to annihilate their imaginary adversaries. It's no different than creating a character and writing about him. To hate someone, most people adopt imaginations of the people they hate as having certain personalities and traits that are worthy of hatred. When they see someone who is wrapped in the skin they've come to hate, they attach the personalities of their imaginary adversaries to the people they see, and this makes it easier for them to launch an attack against those people. What you'll find is that many of the people who were once in hate groups were either reformed in prison or in church. They simply needed to get out and meet people who didn't look, sound or live like them. It's when we begin to discover how similar we are to others that we are able to extend love to those people. For example, a man on a killing spree may be moved by a woman who reminds him of himself. If he knows that she's been hurt the same way he's been hurt, he'll likely spare her life because he can identify with her.

Again, most people hate what they don't understand. Some people hate beggars. They refuse to give them a meal, a blanket or even a cup of coffee because they've developed a perception of beggars. Perception is oftentimes a lie we tell ourselves to justify not liking another human being. We attempt to run away from our compassionate self by poisoning ourselves with lies about others. It helps us to dehumanize others by refusing to hear their stories, so we can continue to listen to the stories we've told ourselves. So, when some people see beggars, they tell themselves that these characters are on drugs or alcohol, and they are therefore justified in not giving any money to them. Needless to say, however, most people who refuse to help a homeless man financially will also refuse to feed him. Let's face it: The man can't snort a cheeseburger. When questioned, most will scream, "He can get up and work just like me!" They do not understand

that the Bible says that we sometimes
entertain angels. Rather than looking at
the man's surface, it is better to look at
his heart. There are homeless people
who've fought in wars for the United
States of America, and many people have
bypassed them as they begged because
to help that hungry man holding up the
sign on the side of the road oftentimes
meant they wouldn't be able to splurge
when they went out for their weekly
shopping trips. Helping the homeless
can oftentimes require self-sacrifice.
You may not be able to get everything
you want, but you will be able to afford
everything you need. But again, most
folks will tell themselves that they are
not going to deprive themselves of the
pleasures of life in order to feed some
"lazy" guy. Let's say that the man who's
been labeled as lazy is a war veteran
whose lost his mind while in war. Let's
say he fought in Vietnam, and while
there, he'd seen and experienced some
things that has changed him forever.

Now, he's nothing more than another
beggar on the streets, ignored, cold and
hungry while people walk past him
carrying their well-fed dogs; dogs who
are wearing sweaters they don't need.
That beggar sits there, using trash cans
to warm himself while so-called
Christians hang stockings for their cats
on their fireplaces. No one cares enough
to try to get to the root of the issue in
that man's life. Many people are
operating in hatred, refusing to feed
their brethren, but they'll go to the zoo
and pay good money to buy a few stems
of lettuce to feed a well-fed giraffe. Many
people who are alive today are like that
nameless rich man in the Bible who
passed by a homeless Lazarus every day,
never reaching out to help him. He was
rich; therefore, he had more than
enough, but he was selfish. Selfishness
and hatred are one and the same. It
means to be so caught up in one's self
that you forget to love your brother as
you love yourself. Anyone who says they

love the LORD, yet the love for their brother is not evident, is a liar and the truth is not in them. I'm sure the rich man who ignored Lazarus would pay for another opportunity to come back to earth to redeem his soul.

Luke 16:19-31: There was a certain rich man, who was clothed in purple and fine linen, and feasted sumptuously every day: And there was a certain beggar named Lazarus, who was laid at his gate, full of sores, And desiring to be fed with the crumbs which fell from the rich man's table: moreover the dogs came and licked his sores. And it came to pass, that the beggar died, and was carried by the Angels into Abraham's bosom: the rich man also died, and was buried; And in Hades he lifted up his eyes, being in torment, and seeing Abraham far off, and Lazarus in his bosom. And he cried and said, Father Abraham, have mercy on me, and send Lazarus, that he may dip the tip of his finger in water, and cool my tongue; for I am tormented in this flame. But Abraham said, Son, remember that you in your lifetime received your good things, and likewise Lazarus evil things: but now he is comforted, and you are tormented. And besides all this, between us and you there is a great gulf fixed: so that they who would pass from here to you cannot; neither can they pass to us, that would come from there. Then he said, I pray you therefore, Father, that you would send him to my Father's house: For I have five Brothers; that he may testify unto them, lest they also come into this place of torment. Abraham said unto him, They have Moses and the prophets; let them hear them. And he said, Nay, Father Abraham: but if one went unto them from the dead, they will repent. And he said unto him, If they hear not Moses and the prophets, neither will they be persuaded, though one rose from the dead.

Hate never benefits a man. Instead, it

steals his joy, success and chance at salvation because hatred is bondage. It is a prison where those who are in it are only fed with barely enough love to share with the people around them. Hate is like a cancer. It eats its host from within and starts to make its ugly presence known by tattooing its madness on their countenances. The core of their eyes seems to darken to bear witness to the devil within.

At some point in your life, you have got to look around you. Think about where your friends' lives are heading. Do you want that future for you and your family? Hate won't take you anywhere, but it will keep you from going places. If you have children, think about them. Wouldn't you like to see them live a life better than the one you have lived?

Unveiling Love

Most people say that love is an emotion.
We were taught in school that love and
hatred are both emotions, but this is not
true. Love is not an emotion, and love is
not a feeling that we get. Love is a spirit,
and that's why the Bible tells us that
love never fails. Just as a spirit cannot
die, but is eternal, love can never fail, for
it is eternal. So just what is love?
Better yet, who is love? GOD is Love, of
course.
1 John 4:8: He that loves not knows not
GOD; for GOD is love.

Because many people don't understand
that love is not an emotion, they
entertain their feelings and identify
those feelings as love. If they truly knew
what they were experiencing, they would
know how to be free from hindering

emotions that masquerade as love. But since most people think that infatuation is love, they engage in it, justify it and laugh at its behaviors.

But just how is GOD love? By telling us that HE is love, GOD is informing us of the very essence of who HE is. 1 Corinthians 13:4-8 gives us a better description of who HE is and what HE stands for.

1 Corinthians 13:4-8: Love is patient, love is kind. It does not envy, it does not boast, it is not proud. It does not dishonor others, it is not self-seeking, it is not easily angered, it keeps no record of wrongs. Love does not delight in evil but rejoices with the truth. It always protects, always trusts, always hopes, always perseveres. Love never fails.

Let's rightly divide the scriptures.
In the biblical description of love, GOD is telling us about HIMSELF, and if HE lives in us, we must see the evidence of HIM

by witnessing that very-same love in ourselves.

Love is patient: How many times have we given up on people and walked away from them? Yet, GOD is patient with us and HE has forgiven us time and time again for our transgressions. HE said that HE would never leave nor forsake us.

Love is kind: We see GOD'S love and kindness through HIS tender mercies. HE is gentle with us, and HE gives us favor, even though we don't deserve it.

Love does not envy: To envy someone means to want to be them or take their place. Love does not envy because love is not self-seeking.

Love does not boast: GOD said we must love our neighbors as we love ourselves. Anytime we boast, we are exalting ourselves above our neighbors and whoever else dares to listen to us.

Love is not proud: Pride is an abomination to GOD. GOD hates a proud look. It is to exalt one's self over others.

We are but dirt; therefore, we have no right to put ourselves on pedestals. After all, GOD does not throw it in our face how undeserving we are of HIS love, grace and attention. Instead, HE just loves us.

Love does not dishonor others: Whomever GOD loves, HE honors. Just as a parent honors their children, GOD honors HIS children. To dishonor someone means to shame or disgrace them. GOD does not do that to us. Instead, HE told us that love covers a multitude of sins. Anytime we set out to disgrace someone else, we are not acting in love; we are acting in selfish ambition, pride, envy or vengeance.

Love is not easily angered: Have you ever been in a relationship with someone you were not truly attracted to? If you were, did you notice how short you were with them? That's because you had no love for them; therefore, you were easily angered by them. But true love is patient, and is not easily angered. GOD is not easily angered with us; after all, HE gives us grace.

Love keeps no records of wrongs: GOD said that HE would forgive us for our sins and remember them no more. HE said HE would toss away our sins in a sea of forgetfulness. Anytime we keep records, we are grabbing for power; a power that belongs to GOD. This behavior is not rooted in love; it is rooted in selfishness.

Love does not delight in evil but rejoices with the truth: The truth has set us free. Love not only hates evil, but it rejoices with the truth, not in the truth. What does this mean? It means that the truth is not something we can enter into. The truth has to enter us, and love will rejoice with the truth. To get a little deeper, the Bible tells us that JESUS CHRIST is the Truth; HE is the living WORD of GOD manifested. All the same, GOD is love; therefore, GOD rejoices with CHRIST, and HE is not delighted with evil.

Love always protects, always trusts, always hopes, always perseveres: GOD has been protecting us since we were formed in our mothers' wombs. HE could have given up on us long ago, but HE patiently waits for us and HE perseveres through our many hurtful decisions. To say that we love someone, we must be protective of them. We must trust that GOD will lead them, and we must hope for the best with and in them.

But now that we know who love is, and how love acts, we must determine whether or not love lives in us. Answer the following questions truthfully.

1. **Have you forgiven your enemies?** Love inhabits forgiveness, but selfishness is the face of unforgiveness.

2. **Would you help your enemies if they needed your help?** Many believers claim to have forgiven their enemies, but when asked if they would help their enemies if

they needed them, their response is oftentimes no. This indicates that they have not truly forgiven their enemies.

3. **Do you feed the homeless when you can?** Feeding the homeless, visiting the prisoners in prison and being compassionate to widows is a showmanship of the GOD who inhabits you. Anyone can say they love the LORD, but the fruit is what will tell you what type of love they are rooted in; whether it be selfishness or agape.

4. **Do you tell others the truth, even when you know the truth won't be welcomed?** On average, most believers withhold the truth from others out of fear of being persecuted, offensive or mistreated. Nevertheless, true love speaks up, but selfishness is a quiet beast when its chain is yanked by fear.

5. **Is the WORD of GOD in you?** In

the beginning was the WORD, and the WORD was with GOD, and the WORD was GOD. This is scriptural; therefore, if the WORD is not in us, how can we love someone seeing that GOD is love?

6. **Do you love the LORD with all of your heart, mind and soul?** Just about everyone who reads this question will say that they love the LORD, but what would GOD say? HE said that these people draw near to HIM with their mouths, but their hearts are far from HIM. HE said if we love HIM, we are to keep HIS commandments. Are you keeping HIS commandments to love HIM with all of your heart and to love your neighbor as you love yourself? Do you honor HIM with your body, your words and your decisions? Your fruit will always speak up on your behalf.

7. **Would you risk your life to save the life of someone else, or does**

that depend on who the person is that needs saving? Love is not selfish or self-seeking. If we love our neighbors as we love ourselves, then we'd risk our lives to save them, and it wouldn't matter who they were.

Whenever we are harmed by some event or events in our lives, the enemy always uses those events to further expose us to evil. As they say, "Hurt people hurt people" (Author unknown).

<u>The Cure For Hatred</u>

It goes without saying that the cure for hatred is love. How nice would it be to walk up to an individual who's imprisoned by hatred and free them up with nothing more than a hug? But in many cases, it's not that simple. As a matter of fact, someone who hates you has already murdered you in their mind. You don't want to get too close to them unless GOD says otherwise.

Here are some tips to help you put a restraining order on hatred in your life.
1. Get to know GOD. In order to love GOD, you have to get to know HIM. To get to know HIM, you must know HIS WORD.
2. Love GOD. You cannot truly love yourself or others without first loving GOD. *"He that loveth not*

177

knowth not God; for God is love" (1 John 4:8).

3. Love GOD'S people. Sure, people can be unlovable at times, but GOD still loves them, so we must do the same. All the same, it is easier to love someone if you confess to yourself and GOD that you are not perfect. *"If a man say, I love God, and hateth his brother, he is a liar: for he that loveth not his brother whom he hath seen, how can he love God whom he hath not seen?"* *(1 John 4:20)*

4. Recognize your hatred, if it's there. Don't keep telling yourself that you don't hate someone when you do. If you think about them a lot and wish the worst for them, then chances are, you are in hatred. Confess how you feel to GOD, renounce hatred and pride, and repent. Ask HIM to change your heart.

5. Forgive quickly. Anytime someone

hurts you, don't allow that pain to sit in you for too long. Speak with them, and if they refuse to repent, take what they did and how you feel about them before the altar of GOD. Leave that situation and your feelings at the altar, and move on.

6. Understand that everyone has free will, and everyone won't come to the LORD nor will they do right by you. One of the hardest lessons to grasp is that the people we love so dearly won't accept CHRIST as their LORD and SAVIOR. Because of this, they won't accept you when you have CHRIST in you. One of the things that helped me to forgive those who hurt me was knowing that they did only what they knew how to do. They didn't have the same convictions as I did, nor did they understand the gravity of what they'd done. They did what they knew how to do, because it

was their normal.

7.   Understand that you may be the very instrument GOD uses to win the souls of the people who hurt you for the Kingdom of GOD. We can never get so wrapped up in ourselves and our own hurts that we forget that these people are living souls who are loved by GOD.

8.   Don't let strife sit on your heart. Strife engages you with yourself until you've become so full of rage that you act upon how you feel. Rather than dealing with the person who hurt you, deal with the strife on the inside of you. *"For where envying and strife is, there is confusion and every evil work"* *(James 3:16).*

9.   Let GOD pick your friends and your spouse. Please understand that Satan is always trying to send one of his own into your life so they can get into your heart. Once there, he will begin to advise them

as to how to treat you. Everyone is not mature enough to be in your heart, for it is a sacred place; one where GOD lives. *"Keep thy heart with all diligence; for out of it are the issues of life" (Proverbs 4:23).*

10. Tell yourself the truth, and accept it. Oftentimes, we fill up on lies because the truth hurts. We should want the truth, however, if we want to live peacefully and without interference. Nevertheless, as human beings, we imagine what we'd like our lives to be like, and then we position the people in our lives to help us get there. When they go outside of what we've expected of them, we find ourselves hurt and angry with them. The truth is...not everyone can have access to you, relative or non-relative. Stop lying to yourself, and position your life around the truth.

11. Confess your sins daily. This is

such a freeing experience, and once you engage in it, you will never want to go another day without confessing. Tell GOD how you feel and what you want. Apologize and repent for anything that is evil, and ask the LORD to help you with your walk in HIM. Tell HIM that you need HIM.

12. Expose yourself to others who are not like you. Don't allow perception to finalize your thinking; get to know the people you've come to judge.

13. Stay away from hateful people. Remember, the WORD of GOD tells us that evil communication ruins useful habits.

14. Stay away from negative news about the person or type of people you've developed an issue with. Try reading up on some positive stories about individuals in that group or listening to positive stories about that particular

individual.

15.   Don't trust everyone. For example, if you're trying to stop hating people of a different race than yourself, it is not wise to just go out and choose any friend in that race. In every race, there are good people and evil people. If you join hands with the first person you meet of that race, you may interlock your fingers with a devil.

16.   Pray about everyone. Ask GOD to drive everyone from your life who shouldn't be in it, and ask HIM to close every demonic access door that's providing demonic traffic to your heart.

17.   Start a love campaign. Try helping someone from the very group or the very individual you've come to hate.

18.   Check yourself often. One of the things I've noticed with people in general is that most people are so busy checking others that they

forget to check themselves. Self reflect and self correct.

19. Try to understand the person or people who have hurt you. Sure, there's no way to justify being wronged by another human being, but the least you could do is understand. The more I spoke with my parents about the things I'd endured growing up, the more I began to get insight into their upbringings. I came to understand that many of their choices reflected choices they'd watched their parents make. They were engaging in generational thinking.

20. Don't let it bother you if the person who's hurt you or the people who've hurt you refuse to apologize. With GOD, there's order, and the first order of business, as commanded by HIM, is to confront the person or people you have a problem with before coming to HIM. *"Therefore if thou*

bring thy gift to the altar, and there
rememberest that thy brother hath
ought against thee; Leave there
thy gift before the altar, and go thy
way; first be reconciled to thy
brother, and then come and offer
thy gift" (Matthew 5:23-24). If the
person or people refuse to
apologize, the next order of
business is to forgive them. To
forgive means to give the situation
to GOD. GOD will take it from
there.

Of course, one of the most obvious and
effective ways to cure hatred in the earth
is to spray it with love. Then again, we
have to be aware of the fact that some
people will continue to choose hatred,
even after being exposed to love. The
prison systems don't encourage love,
and when someone finds love or
reformation from within a prison, it is a
miraculous move of GOD. Most people
go to prison and serve out their time.

They are being made to pay for their crimes, which is good, of course, but we should also rehabilitate the prisoners while they are incarcerated. We do this by loving and educating them. Telling a prisoner that they are nothing more than waste upon the earth and then giving them more rights than you give a victim ensures that they will continue their crimes against mankind. We know this when raising children. If you have a child and you don't show love to that child, yet you are protective of that child, that child will grow up to be a menace to society. That child will be confused and learn to seek attention, be it negative or positive attention. Your child's behavior would be nothing more than attention-seeking tantrums designed to get you to finally see him or her. That's what criminals do. Their behaviors are oftentimes tantrums. You'll notice that many offenders are repeat offenders. Many offenders are simply overgrown children who are repeatedly crying out for help through their very actions. In many neighborhoods, the police are the only positive role models some boys have. The mothers have to call the police to come over and correct their sons because their fathers are either incarcerated or in the streets somewhere doing things worthy of incarceration. Officers build relationships with these boys, where they have to be the firm, male figure in their lives. How could we cure this? It's simple. If we'd only open up our hearts to those who are hurting around us, we'd see a change, but nowadays, it's every man for himself. You don't have to invite some brokenhearted boy into your home. I can understand how that could be scary, but if every positive man and woman took a child under their wings, we'd see more positive adults in the next generation. Right now, we see crime and we see criminals, but we don't see the backgrounds of where these criminals are coming from.

How did I get delivered from that pain
that raised me? As I grew and hungered
more and more for GOD, I gave in to that
hunger and fed myself with the WORD.
In the beginning, it was slow. I read the
Bible and went to the church (building)
sometimes, but I always lived as I wanted
to. The more WORD came in me, the
more hatred and unforgiveness came out
of me. I began to love the people who'd
victimized me because I was, and am, no
longer a victim of their acts. You see,
when you are still in victim mode, you
are always looking to harm or see harm
come upon the people who've victimized
you. But when you forgive, you are only
looking to see them get delivered from
the hurt that caused them to do what
they did to you in the first place. Even if
deliverance is brought on by tribulation,
you want them to get it right because
GOD loves them despite their crimes
against you, just like HE loves you
despite your crimes against others and
HIM.

We can look at the surface, and we can look at the stem, but it takes a mighty man or woman of GOD to see and reach into the soil and pull up the root of hatred. Once that root is gone, we are relocated to a holy place where we can grow up in the right things and be replanted, renewed, retried and watered with an everlasting spring of life.

I have a system that I found has worked for me, and I've seen many live by this very same system. With the people who have wronged me, I prayed and asked the LORD to put forgiveness in me for them and HE did. Then I made a conscious effort to stay away from them and people like them. Some people will say to you, "Baby, family is family. No matter what, y'all need to stick together 'cause nobody will love you like family." That's a lie from the pits of hell! If someone could possibly push you to relapse on drugs, what does the rehab center advise that you do? Stay away from them, because you may very well get delivered and start living a normal, healthy, happy, GOD-filled life when all of a sudden, that family member could cause you to relapse and pick up that old mindset. We must understand that we need a certain mindset to deal with certain people. We are related in the natural to our relatives when we are born, but once we are born again, the Blood of JESUS makes us a new creature. We are then, therefore, no longer related to those who do not serve HIM.

Matthew 12:48-50: But he answered and said unto him that told him, Who is my mother? and who are my brethren? And he stretched forth his hand toward his disciples, and said, Behold my mother and my brethren! For whosoever shall do the will of my Father which is in heaven, the same is my brother, and sister, and mother.

If you associate yourself with evil people, expect evil things to happen. If you associate yourself with evil people, you will become evil yourself.

1 Corinthians 15:33: Be not deceived: evil companions corrupt good morals.

Think of how an infectious disease works. If you sit near a man with the flu, you will likely catch the flu from him. If you hang out with someone who's infected with foolishness, you will likely pick up foolishness from him.

Proverbs 13:20: He that walketh with wise men shall be wise: but a companion of fools shall be destroyed.

Imagine this: A man named Darren goes out job hunting and gets hired at this big accounting firm. He's excited because this is a boost to his resume. His future is looking bright, and now he has the chance to break the chains of poverty that have held his family captive, generation by generation. He quickly ascends the ranks, becoming a hiring manager in no time and doubling his pay.

For him, life is good. He has a beautiful
wife who loves him, two beautiful
children, and the house of his dreams.
GOD has surely blessed him.

One day, a familiar face walks into the
office for an interview. His name is
Robert Smith. Initially, Darren had
called Robert to come in for an interview,
but he did not realize that the man was
the Robert Smith he knew. After all,
Robert Smith is a common name. Robert
Smith is Darren's long-time enemy.
Robert spent his whole childhood
making sure Darren's childhood was a
nightmare. Even as a teen, Robert didn't
ease his bullying and oppressive ways.
He stole Darren's girlfriends, tried to
attack Darren's sister and cursed out
Darren's mother. Now, Robert is sitting
there in a suit and tie looking at Darren,
hoping to get hired. When he sees
Darren, however, he knows his chances
of getting hired are almost non-existent,
outside of the power of GOD. You see,

Robert repented years ago. His dad used to make him feel like he wasn't man enough, so Robert had taken his pain out on Darren since he saw that Darren had a doting father and seemed to have everything. Plus, Robert's mother was deceased. He wanted to be Darren's friend, but since Darren was so happy and wasn't into all of the things he was into (home burglaries, girl harassing and smoking marijuana), he decided that he would try to instill fear in Darren. This way, he could control the boy he envied. Again, Robert got saved three years ago. He has always wanted to see Darren to apologize, but not like this.

Darren is beside himself. Here is his opportunity to exact revenge on the face that made his life miserable. Even though Robert is the best and most qualified applicant for the job posted, he tells Robert, "We'll call you." Robert is heartbroken and leaves in tears. He has been paying for his choices for years and just wants the chance to make them right. He goes home to his wife and six children to tell them that the job didn't come through, and they will probably have to move into a shelter for a little while; nevertheless, Darren is overcome with happiness. He takes a lunch break and calls his wife to tell her about how the infamous Robert Smith came into his office begging him for a job. Darren is walking around downtown, not paying attention, just elated with the day's events. His wife, being the voice of reason, tries to tell him how wrong he is, but he doesn't want to hear it. This was an opportunity of a lifetime, and he is thrilled to have had it. While Darren is walking, he doesn't look both ways to see that car speeding down the road, trying to elude the police. He's struck by the elusive driver and dies instantly. Darren is carried away to hell, where everlasting torment awaits him. Meanwhile, Robert gets another call from the firm since they now have an opening for hiring manager. They offer him Darren's old spot and Robert works there for 40 years before he retires, dying at the ripe old age of 93. When he dies, he's carried off to Heaven.

Do you understand what happened there? Darren was still bound by unforgiveness. Even though GOD had blessed him and given him a chance to repent and move forward, he chose to play GOD. In the midst of his happiness, he got tested and failed when he decided that Robert did not deserve a second chance. On the other hand, Robert was free for a while. He'd repented and was truly sorry for what he'd done, and he wanted a chance to make it right again. Like all of us, Darren committed many crimes (sins) against the LORD and the LORD'S people. Even though he'd repented for what he'd done, he decided that he would not forgive someone who'd once hurt him. This crime in itself is unforgivable because GOD has forgiven us for our many transgressions against HIM, but when we can't extend that same grace to another person, we step outside of GOD'S likeness (resemblance) and begin to look more like HIS enemy.

One of the most powerful demonstrations of unforgiveness is the story of the wicked servant told by CHRIST.

Matthew 18:21-35: Then came Peter to him, and said, Lord, how often shall my Brother sin against me, and I forgive him? till seven times?

Jesus said unto him, I say not unto you, Until seven times: but, Until seventy times seven. Therefore is the kingdom of heaven likened unto a certain king, who would take account of his servants. And when he had begun the reckoning, one was brought unto him, who owed him ten thousand talents. But since he had nothing to pay, his lord commanded him to be sold, and his wife, and children, and all that he had, and payment to be made. The servant therefore fell down, and worshiped him, saying, Lord, have patience with me, and I will pay you all. Then the lord of that servant was moved with compassion, and released him, and forgave him the debt. But the same servant went out, and found one of his fellow servants, who owed him a hundred pence: and he laid hands on him, and took him by the throat, saying, Pay me what you owe. And his fellow servant fell down at his feet, and besought him, saying, Have patience with me, and I will pay you all. And he would not: but went and cast him into prison, till he should pay the debt. So when his fellow servants saw what was done, they were very sorry, and came and told unto their lord all that was done. Then his lord, after that he had called him, said unto him, O you wicked servant, I forgave you all that debt, because you desired me: Should not you also have had compassion on your fellow servant, even as I had pity on you? And his lord was angry, and delivered him to the jailers, till he should pay all that was due unto him. So likewise shall my heavenly Father do also unto you, if you from your hearts forgive not everyone his Brother their trespasses.

To Hell With Hate

Growing up, I had (and still have) a love for animals in me that really impacted my life. One day, when I was around eleven or twelve-years-old, I heard the sounds of a dog screaming. I could tell he was in pain, and I could hear what sounded like a stick or large object beating on something. I noticed that the dog's screams coincided with every bang I heard. It was nighttime, and my parents and I were just arriving home and heading into the house. As I heard the dog's screams, I began to cry. I knew someone was beating him to death, and I could not stand it. I wanted to go and find the poor puppy, but I couldn't. It was dark outside and I couldn't tell where the sounds were originating from. I sat in the house and cried, and I just hoped for the dog's sake that he'd pass away so he wouldn't have to endure that pain anymore. I remember wishing I had had a gun to kill the person who I believed to be killing a defenseless animal.

As I grew up, that memory never faded. It continued to haunt me over the years because I could remember so vividly that dog's screams of agony.

Nowadays, I don't wish I could have killed the guy who was killing the dog. I wish I could have rescued that dog somehow and had that character arrested. Needless to say, as wicked as that man was, he was and is still loved by GOD. That man or boy had a story. Why do I assume it was a guy? Because of the amount of force I could hear being exhibited. Needless to say, if that character has not repented and continues to live a life of hatred, he will open his eyes one day and realize he's in hell.

Hell is not a place designed for mankind.
Hell was created for Satan and his
angels, but the same sentence GOD gave
to the fallen angels is a spoken Word
that has gone forth from GOD, and as
such, mankind falls under that sentence.
Satan knew that if man sinned, he'd be
hell-bound, and that's why he tempted
Eve in the Garden of Eden. Satan is the
great accuser of the brethren. He wanted
to see if GOD would follow through with
HIS WORD because Satan and his angels
were condemned to hell. Nevertheless,
GOD judged Adam and Eve for biting into
the fruit and disobeying HIM, but HE
issued a blow to Satan's pride when HE
told him that HE would send HIS Son to
redeem mankind. HE would offer up HIS
only begotten Son as a sin offering for
man. That's why Satan hates you so
much. You were given a second chance.
GOD not only created you in HIS image,
but HE also sent HIS Son to redeem your
soul from the very place HE'D
condemned Satan and his angels to. In

other words, you are loved, so there is
no reason for you to hate anyone.

After all I'd been through as a young
woman, I had every reason to hate
others...if we measure my pain by human
standards. But it was GOD'S love that
changed me. It was the love of GOD that
drew me. You see, having been through
so much pain, humiliation and betrayal
taught me to look past a person's flesh
to see the wounds on their soul. I can
empathize with the heartbroken, judged,
misguided rebel. One day, I found myself
telling a girl that I'd rather be found
dining with lost souls who knew they
were lost than to be found dining with
religious souls who thought they were
found. I'd rather share the love of GOD
with them, and try to reach into the
darkness and be that light that brings
them to CHRIST than to sit at a table
with a bunch of self-righteous, religious
prunes whose only concern was making
sure their wigs didn't blow off. That's

when the LORD began to bring to my
remembrance how CHRIST lived and
loved mankind. HE wasn't found at the
table with the Pharisees and Sadducees.
HE was found at the table with sinners
and tax collectors who wanted to hear
the WORD of GOD.

Nowadays, I live a GOD-filled life, and I
am truly thankful for everything I've
been through, and I say that with the
purest sincerity. I'm thankful because
my pain helped me to locate others who
are in pain and lead them to CHRIST.
Truthfully, I haven't shared even ten
percent of what I have been through as a
child and woman, but if I can get through
it all and still learn to love again, so can
you.

As a human being, you were created in
the likeness of GOD, and you are loved
by your FATHER. It doesn't matter what
you've done, HE still loves you. You
don't have to go to hell and spend your

eternity with a bunch of people and devils who abandoned love for selfishness. No one who hates another person will enter Heaven. If I'd given in to the pain and allowed myself to be a hateful force upon the face of the earth, the devil would have won twice. He would have won at hurting me while on earth, and he would have been successful in getting my soul to hell. I chose to let him lose twice. Instead of letting all I've been through define me, I gave that pain to GOD and HE healed me. HE then gave me new knowledge, new revelation, wisdom and understanding, and I was able to take these beautiful jewels to those who were like me.

One day, I posted on Facebook about some of what I've been through because I am no longer ashamed of my testimony. So many people messaged me because they'd also been through a lot of what I'd been through, but had been ashamed to admit it. All of a sudden, one of the females in ministry posted up a status condemning people for using their pain as their ministry. She then went on to say that she didn't have a testimony, but she still had the WORD. I wanted to be quiet, but I knew her status was a direct response to my status about what I'd gone through. I wrote her back telling her not to condemn others or try to quiet their stories, for the WORD tells us to testify about what we've endured. All the same, my ministry isn't built on my hurt, nor is it "my" ministry; it is the ministry of JESUS CHRIST, and GOD still continues to tell us about what CHRIST suffered for us on the cross. Should we tell HIM to quiet that part of HIS story so that we could have matching ministries? No. Whatever the devil did to you, shout it from the rooftops to let him know that he did not win. You will overcome him with your testimony. *"And they overcame him by the blood of the Lamb, and by the word of their testimony; and they loved not their lives unto death"*

(Revelation 12:11). The devil likes to keep you quiet because it is then that he can keep you bound.

There are many people on the earth who'd silence you if they could, but why take all of that hurt, pain, and those memories to hell with you when you can cast that burden upon the LORD, live life with a smile and still go to Heaven?

Hell No, We Won't Go

One night more than a decade ago, I
dreamed that I was in hell. I was walking
around and there were no people there,
nor was there any fire. For years, I did
not understand that dream, but now I do.
Because hell was not designed for me, I
could not experience it. Obviously, I was
there illegally, so the fires of hell could
not come against me nor could they
terrorize me. I only saw what appeared
to be the interior of a red-like cave, and I
knew I was in hell, but I didn't
understand where everyone was.

Hell wasn't designed for you or me. It
was designed for Satan and his angels. I
don't care if you're tattooed all over,
cursing in every sentence you speak and
drinking your life away. GOD still loves
you and HE desires for you to reach into

HIS redeeming hand so HE can save you. CHRIST is the bridge to Heaven. Don't throw your life away looking for "fun" when joy is so much greater. Don't waste another second hating another human being. No man or woman is worth going to hell for. You may think that in hating someone, you are punishing them, but you aren't. The greatest punishment you can issue to a person who has hurt you is to love them even after they've wronged you. Then, to add insult to injury, anytime you continue forth in the LORD and let GOD bless you, you cause GOD to seat your enemies at a table where HE intends to honor you in their presence.

Psalm 23:5: You prepare a table before me in the presence of my enemies; You anoint my head with oil; my cup overflows.

Think about it: Going to hell to show someone how much you hate them is as pointless as driving off a cliff to show someone how much you love them.

One day, I began to reflect back over my life, the things I'd been through and the choices I've made. I'd just gotten off the phone with another young woman who was going through a really rough trial. Suddenly, I began to smile, and I understood why I'd gone through everything I had. GOD has blessed me to talk someone out of committing suicide and to unknowingly stop someone from aborting their baby, and HE continues to use me to this day. I don't care what someone tells me they've been through in their attempts to justify being mad at GOD or mad at someone else, I always seem to have a testimony that matches theirs. Nowadays, I can listen to someone's story and smile because I know I can reach them, if GOD has graced me to do so. I realize that my pain was not in vain. GOD used what I'd gone through to bring others to HIM. So, if I could go through it all again, would I do it? Of course! Because I survived it all, and GOD gave me the strength to survive it all. I could have used my stories as a justification to go out and sin, but instead, GOD blessed me with the opportunity to share my story to justify HIS WORD. HE is faithful, and HE loves us all.

GOD chose me to do a work in the earth before I entered my mother's womb. My family was so far into sin and wrongful thinking that it would take a miracle to get me to where I needed to be, and a miracle is what GOD gave me. All of the hurt I'd been through as a child was definitely inflicted on me by Satan. His plan was to destroy me, or at least cause me to hurt others, and for a while I fell into the enemy's snare. But no matter how bad I was hurt or how far I went into sin, GOD never left me nor did HE forsake me. HE protected me all those years. There were many times that I could have lost my life, but GOD gave the enemy the same restrictions he'd given to him when he attacked Job. He could touch my body, but he could not touch my life. GOD knew that HE'D raise me up one day to help broken souls find their way back to HIM. In the midst of it all, HIS grace kept me. HIS grace kept me when I was born with a hole in my heart, and the enemy thought he was going to take me out before my journey even began. HIS grace kept me when at two years old, I picked up a pot of boiling hot peaches in sugar and tried to pull it off the table. I still have the scars to prove that HE kept me. HIS grace kept me when I was 19 years old, drunk off gin for the first time, and I handed my car keys to the very people who called themselves my friends. HIS grace kept me when I woke up the next day in a strange vehicle not knowing how I had gotten there, with nothing more than a memory of people asking me where I lived. HIS grace kept me when I'd fallen into the river and was pulled out just

before my head was fully submerged.
His grace kept me when a man I called
"friend" was so set on raping me that he
could have choked the life out of me.
HIS grace kept me when I was looking
for love between the sheets with
"boyfriends." HE could have gotten tired
of me and given up on me, but even
though I'd given up on myself plenty of
times, HE still kept me. HIS grace kept
me through two miscarriages. As a
matter of fact, HE'D warned me the
nights before I miscarried each time in a
dream, showing me in one dream that
my daughter was carried to Heaven by an
Angel. HIS grace kept me when I was
running for my life from a man who'd
sworn to love and honor me for the rest
of his life. HIS grace kept me when my
ex's sister was playing with black magic
and thought she could overcome me, a
child of the MOST HIGH GOD. GOD
laughed at her every time she chanted,
and every time she tried to send devils
out against me. Instead, GOD sent them

right back her way. They couldn't touch me! HIS grace kept me when I was nothing but a fool, chasing behind lust trying to find the one thing I'd always wanted: love. I didn't realize it then, but I had it all along. GOD is love, and HE loved me even when I did not know how to love myself. HIS grace kept me when I couldn't find a group to fit into. I wasn't low enough for the down and out, and I wasn't high enough for the high-minded, but I was just where GOD wanted me to be.

What about you? We like to complain about having been through so much, but the problem with most people is that they see what GOD didn't do for them, but they refuse to see what HE did do. Satan recruits members for his army by hurting them, and that's why GOD said that we can become weary, but we should not faint. What about you? Instead of talking about what a person has taken you through, ask yourself what GOD has brought you through. Every attack that you've ever endured was not launched by GOD; it came from the enemy, but I'll say to you what GOD said to me when I thought I was at my breaking point. HE said to me, "You're strong enough." The same goes for you. You're strong enough to push past hatred and love again. You're strong enough to take everything Satan has tried to do to you and turn it all into a testimony. You're strong enough to love again, even when you've been wronged. I've been betrayed twice, but the men didn't betray me; I betrayed myself by thinking that I could find a blessing in sin. Nevertheless, I haven't given up on marriage. As a matter of fact, I'm more excited about the idea of marriage now because I know I will NEVER choose my own husband again. Either GOD chooses for me or I will never remarry. I trust HIM that much, and I don't trust myself at all. What about you? Have your lessons led you to any blessings? You see, a lot of people get mad when they've gone through something and end up going to fight on the wrong side of the war. They take up their places with the very devil who attacked them in the first place.

I am a living testimony that GOD can bring a broken, dirty and miserable soul into HIS perfect light. HE mended my soul, HE restored me, HE cleansed me, and above all, HE saved me. After all of the hell I've been through on earth, I couldn't even fathom what the real hell must look like. And to think, as much as I've gone through, I haven't been through half of what some people have. Nevertheless, I am satisfied with my portion, and that's why I never covet anyone's anointing. I don't know the price of the oil that was extracted from them, and I wouldn't want to experience their trials. It was hard enough being me.

So what's your divine instruction?

1. Stop being a victim. The WORD tells us that we are more than conquerors through CHRIST JESUS. Satan wants us to be victims because hurt people hurt people. Choose to use his own weapon against him. Choose to take the pain that you've endured and let GOD turn it into a testimony.

2. Stop looking at where you are and start focusing on where GOD has called you to be. All too often, believers get so caught up in what they can see that they end up forfeiting their blessings. Remember, you can't see the future, but that doesn't mean it won't eventually come to pass.

3. Stop worrying about judgmental people. I've learned that in life, there are many cliques, but each clique represents a different type of mindset. We often draw nearest to the people who think like us,

and we are often rejected by the people who can't relate to us. In my life, I've had to come face-to-face with the fact that I just don't fit in, and that's because I wasn't created to fit in; I was created to stand out. Judgmental people are judged people. Their portions are already awaiting them, and many times, you'll find that their lives are nothing more than pathetic reruns of generational mindsets.

4. Stop letting people devalue you. Do you realize how far you have to step down from being a prince or princess of the Kingdom of GOD just to fit into some man or woman's idea of what you should be? It's really an insult, if you think about it.

5. Stop undervaluing yourself. You are worth more than you realize. If you took your greatest imagination and measured it up to GOD'S plan for you, you'd be amazed at how

much you've discounted yourself.

6. Stop blaming GOD. GOD didn't hurt you, and I know many people like to say that HE didn't protect them, but the truth is: HE did. GOD is still the same GOD who condemned Satan to hell, but not before telling him that HE'D send a Redeemer for you. If you survived something, it's because GOD gave you the strength to survive it, but it's up to you what you do with that lesson. Will you help someone else who's suffering through what you've suffered or will you keep it all in and self-destruct?

7. Take some time each day and speak with the LORD. Set up a scheduled time each day to have a one-on-one conversation with HIM. HE wants to hear from you, and as soon as you get in HIS will, HE will explain why you've gone through what you've gone through and how

you got through it.

8. Take some time each day to read the Bible. You'd be amazed at how much your life will change if you'll only read one chapter a day every day for a year.

9. Get away from people who think they know your value, but don't. Just like the wrong romantic partner can be deadly to your destiny, the wrong friend can be deadly to your destiny. One thing I've witnessed in life is that every time I tried to break out of a mindset, I had a friend still in that mindset who didn't want to see me go. I've offended plenty of friends by simply stepping outside of their understandings and stepping into GOD'S will for my life. Needless to say, they are no longer friends.

10. Didn't GOD tell you HE'D set a place for you in the presence of your enemies? Don't you realize that you need enemies to push you

to the next level? Besides, if you didn't have enemies, who'd be there to witness GOD set that place for you? Learn to disappoint your enemies by loving the hell out of them....literally.

Understanding Heaven & Hell

We've all been told about the pearly gates of Heaven, and we've all been told about the dreaded gates of hell. We've heard about Heaven's beauty and many of the blessings we'll experience living there. At the same time, we've heard about the hideousness of hell, and many of the agonies its residents will be subjected to for eternity. The amazing thing about the human mind, however, is that it cannot comprehend the word "eternity", nor can it comprehend "unbearable torture." That's why it's so easy for atheism and agnosticism to become such widespread doctrines. We know that GOD is a GOD of love; therefore, it's hard to fathom the idea that HE'D condemn someone HE loves to an eternity of torture. Even as a believer, we still find this truth hard to understand; nevertheless, we know it to be true.

Many believers end up turning away from the truth because the world's doctrine allows its followers to indulge in the pleasures of this world without fear of an eternal punishment. People often seek this doctrine because of the strong, unquenchable desires of the flesh. After all, we've been taught by our parents to nurture our flesh and to give in to its desires. The thought of neglecting ourselves and living in holiness, a lifestyle that is completely foreign to us, is almost incomprehensible. For this reason, it is easier to believe the lie than it is to believe the truth. But to understand the truth, we must go all the way back to the first rebellious act committed against GOD.

We all know the story of how Lucifer (Satan) came to be cast out of Heaven. He coveted GOD'S position. He wanted to be worshipped; he wanted to be GOD.

Lucifer led a rebellion in Heaven, and the Bible tells us that one third of the angels revolted with him against GOD. Because of their revolt, GOD kicked them out of Heaven and judged them. HE condemned Satan and his angels (demons/ devils) to an eternity in hell. GOD'S declaration wasn't limited, however. GOD'S declaration meant that all living things that revolted against HIM would be sentenced to an eternity in hell. The earth is the LORD'S and the fullness thereof, so hell was a place created or set apart for Satan and his angels. That was the original purpose for hell.

Revelation 12:7-9: And there was war in heaven: Michael and his angels fought against the dragon; and the dragon fought and his angels, And prevailed not; neither was their place found any more in heaven. And the great dragon was cast out, that old serpent, called the Devil, and Satan, which deceiveth the whole world: he was cast out into the earth, and his angels were cast out with him.

When GOD created Adam, HE made him
in HIS image; this means that HE made
Adam in HIS likeness. But HE took Eve
from the rib of Adam, making her in
Adam's likeness. This meant that Eve
was a little lower than Adam. Remember,
in the Kingdom of GOD, there is rank,
but a higher rank with GOD doesn't
mean that one is loved greater than the
other; it simply means that someone is
given greater responsibility than the
other. Satan knew it would be easier to
tempt Eve than it was to tempt Adam, so
he told her that if she ate of the tree that
GOD had forbidden her and Adam from
eating from, she would receive the
greatest rank that there was. He told her
that she would be as a god; she would be
like GOD. In other words, Satan tempted
Eve with the very crime he had been
found guilty of: envy. Satan knew GOD
had already condemned any life that
revolted against HIM to hell, so his place

was to get Adam and Eve to go to hell
with him. He knew that Adam and Eve
were GOD'S beloved. After Eve bit into
that fruit, she bit into judgment. She
then took that fruit to Adam, and he bit
into judgment. This means they were
condemned the very moment they
disobeyed GOD.

After GOD confronted Adam and Eve
about their betrayal, HE judged them,
gave them a new set of laws and cast
them out of the Garden of Eden. But
GOD issued one final blow to Satan's
ego. Satan knew that if Adam and Eve
were full of sin and judgment that every
child born to them, their children and
throughout all generations would be hell
bound. After all, we create after our own
likeness; that's how GOD created us.
Anything that is born of us or to us is
under us, and therefore, like us.
The final blow came when GOD told
Satan that HE would send a Redeemer to
redeem mankind from his sins. In other

words, mankind would get the second chance that Satan could not get. For this reason, Satan hates us with such an intensity that he'll go as far as he can to kill, steal or destroy us.

But here's the issue. Sin is in the earth, and GOD has pre-ordained a time to judge the world, just as HE'D preset a time for the enemy and his angels to go to hell. So, for the meantime, we live in a sin-filled earth with sinners and devils, but just like Adam and Eve, we are protected from the curse of the law, as well as devils as long as we stay in CHRIST. GOD gave us an order, and this order protects us from Satan and his angels; it also protects us from the Old Testament law which condemned us. The order is: GOD is the head of CHRIST, CHRIST is the head of man, and man is the head of woman. This is our Garden of Eden for the time being. We were first to accept JESUS CHRIST as our LORD and Savior, confess HIM as our LORD and Savior, and get baptized to reflect the going down of the dead man and the rising up of the new man. We were raised again in CHRIST JESUS, but those who do not give themselves to GOD or believe upon the CHRIST are still seated in condemnation. Therefore, they are still labeled unbelievers and are not allowed into the protective gardens that GOD has created for every man who believed upon the second Adam: Jesus (Emmanuel). Emmanuel means "GOD with us." So when someone says something like, "If GOD is love, then why would HE send people to a place to burn for all eternity?", the correct way to respond is by reminding them that GOD provided us a way to escape eternal damnation. HE gave us JESUS CHRIST, who reminds us that HE is the way, the truth and the life, and no man comes to the FATHER except through HIM. So the real argument that most people have is: Why isn't there another way? The flesh is strong and it desires to have its own way, and that's why GOD forewarned us about the evilness of our flesh. When we were saved, it was our spirit that was renewed, but our flesh has no inheritance. Our flesh still wants to go by its own laws, and therefore, our struggle to do right and wrong is found in our flesh. The flesh still lusts after people, the flesh still covets after things, and the flesh still wages war against the WORD. We have to realize that we are not our flesh. We are spirit beings wrapped in flesh, and we have to lead our flesh and not be led of it. Hatred is the flesh's reaction to not getting what it wants. Hate is also the flesh's reaction to being mishandled.

Galatians 5:16-24: This I say then, Walk in the Spirit, and ye shall not fulfil the lust of the flesh. For the flesh lusteth against the Spirit, and the Spirit against the flesh: and these are contrary the one to the other: so that ye cannot do the things that ye would. But if ye be led of the Spirit, ye are not under the law. Now the works of the flesh are manifest, which are these; Adultery, fornication, uncleanness, lasciviousness, idolatry, witchcraft, hatred, variance, emulations, wrath, strife, seditions, heresies, envyings, murders, drunkenness, revellings, and such like: of the which I tell you before, as I have also told you in time past, that they which do such things shall not inherit the kingdom of God. But the fruit of the Spirit is love, joy, peace, longsuffering, gentleness, goodness, faith, meekness, temperance: against such there is no law. And they that are Christ's have crucified the flesh with the affections and lusts.

What exactly is Heaven, then? Heaven is GOD'S throne.
Acts 7:49: Heaven is my throne, and earth is my footstool: what house will ye build me? saith the Lord: or what is the place of my rest?
Matthew 23:22: And he that shall swear by heaven, sweareth by the throne of

God, and by him that sitteth thereon.
1 Kings 22:19: And he said, Hear thou
therefore the word of the LORD: I saw
the LORD sitting on his throne, and all
the host of heaven standing by him on
his right hand and on his left.

Where exactly is Heaven, then? Heaven
is in the presence of GOD; therefore,
anytime you say you are going to
Heaven, you are saying that you will
reside in the perfect peace and presence
of GOD. In HIS presence, there will be
no more sorrow or tears, for sin cannot
abound in HIS presence. When GOD
kicked Satan and his angels out of
Heaven, HE was casting them out of HIS
presence.
Luke 10:18: And he said unto them, I
beheld Satan as lightning fall from
heaven.

Even though Satan and his team were
cast out of Heaven, they still have to
present themselves to GOD. Their time

in the earth is limited, and they know this; nevertheless, they still tremble in the presence of GOD, and they still bow to HIM because HE is GOD. They know HE is GOD, but their goal is to convince others that HE doesn't exist.

Job 1:6-7: Now there was a day when the sons of God came to present themselves before the LORD, and Satan came also among them. And the LORD said unto Satan, Whence comest thou? Then Satan answered the LORD, and said, From going to and fro in the earth, and from walking up and down in it.

Getting back to Heaven (the presence of GOD) requires that we bring Heaven (GOD'S dominion) into our hearts, for it is not our physical man that will be saved; it is our spirit man. That's why we are now the temples of the HOLY SPIRIT. We are a sacred people; we are GOD'S dwelling place. For this reason, we must clean up our temples (hearts) of anything that is unlike GOD. GOD will not reside with hatred, nor will HE reside with any forms of ungodliness, for HE is holy. Light and darkness cannot cohabitate, so if we want to get to Heaven, we have to let the WORD evict all of the hell we've allowed inside of us. Hatred is always damned to hell, for it is the very opposite of GOD. Hatred wars against GOD and HIS purpose, so we have a choice to make: Go to Heaven in love or go to hell with hate.

I think back to when I was dealing with the second ex-husband and his sister had made it clear that I was not welcome in her home. That declaration wasn't necessary because I'd already settled it in my heart that I'd never step foot into her house again. Because of all she'd done against me and my marriage, and because I wasn't welcome in her house, I refused to allow her into my house. It wasn't revenge; it was more-so of me not wanting what was in her to visit my dwelling place. Let's think back to GOD.

HE wants to live in our hearts, right? If we don't let Heaven dwell on the inside of us, we won't be dwelling in Heaven. You can't be on both teams and expect to claim the victory from whichever side has the victory. We (believers) already have the victory in CHRIST JESUS, and there is no such thing as a partial Christian. You are either for HIM or against HIM, but there is no place for the neutral to stand except alongside unbelievers.